D0721611

On Track

The Railway Mail Service in Canada

Susan McLeod O'Reilly

National Postal Museum
Canadian Museum of Civilization
and
Canada Post Corporation

© 1992 Canadian Museum of Civilization

Canadian Cataloguing in Publication Data

McLeod O'Reilly, Susan, 1955-

On track: the railway mail service in Canada

Issued also in French under the title:

À fond de train - Le service postal ferroviaire au Canada
ISBN 0-660-90559-0
DSS cat. no. MAS NM98-3/80-1992F
Publié par le Musée canadien des civilisations en collaboration avec le Musée national de la poste et la Société canadienne des postes.

Includes bibliographical references.
ISBN 0-660-14005-5

1. Railway mail service – Canada – History.
2. Postal service – Canada – History.
I. Canadian Museum of Civilization.
II. National Postal Museum (Canada).
III. Canada Post Corporation.
IV. Title.
V. Title: The railway mail service in Canada.

HE6175.M34 1992   383.4971   C92-099720-1

DSS cat. no. NM89-3/80-1992E

PRINTED IN CANADA BY T & H PRINTERS.

Published by the
Canadian Museum of Civilization
Hull, Quebec
J8X 4H2

in cooperation with

The National Postal Museum and
Canada Post Corporation

Credits

Managing Editor / Text Editor:
Julie Swettenham

Designed by:
Purich Design Studio

Production:
Deborah Brownrigg

Cover photograph:

The first train to travel from
Montréal to the Pacific Coast, 1886

*Courtesy of the National Archives of
Canada (PA 66579)*

Back cover photograph: Claire Dufour

Canadä

Table of Contents

Acknowledgements

I would like to acknowledge the contributions made by some special people to the realization of this book:

Francine Brousseau, Manager of the National Postal Museum, steadfastly backed my vision of this book and provided the necessary resources to accomplish the project.

John Willis, my colleague at the National Postal Museum, carefully read the draft manuscript and contributed many helpful comments.

Tom Hillman, archivist for the Post Office Department records at the National Archives of Canada, kindly shared with me the fruits of his research on the early appearance of mail cars.

Bianca Gendreau, assistant curator at the National Postal Museum, diligently tracked down footnotes, photographs and copyright information.

Julie Swettenham, editor at the Canadian Museum of Civilization, worked tirelessly and conscientiously to strengthen the organization of my thoughts and the power of my words, and never missed a deadline!

The former railway clerks deserve special thanks, for their recollections instilled the otherwise technical subject of the railway mail service with a colour and verisimilitude that I hope this work has managed, at least in part, to capture.

Finally, my colleagues on the core project team for the **On Track** exhibition should be praised for having realized such a successful display. In doing so, they provided the impetus for this book. In addition to myself as curator, the team was composed of Francine Brousseau as project leader, Maryse Tellier as educator, and Jean-Pierre Camus as designer.

Walker

Helen

St. Thérèse
de Blair

GRAND TRUNK R.W.
A
UP
MAY 10
1858.

QUEBEC
AUG 9
1854
L.C.

CANADA
CANADA-10-Cts.

6

Capt. Saml. White
Pass

Dear Reader:

When was the last time you mailed something?

Recently, no doubt.

How do you feel when there's no mail for you?

Forgotten, maybe?

Amid a world of telephones, couriers and facsimile machines, we still rely on the Post Office. But a century or two ago the post was all people had. In a land as vast and sparsely populated as Canada, a system for sending messages and goods was essential. First using stagecoach, canoe and dog team, then steamship and train, the Post Office followed newcomers as they settled this country. So necessary, in fact, is the Post Office, that its early history parallels Canada's.

The National Postal Museum is dedicated to the study of postal communication. By collecting, preserving and researching the heritage and material culture of the postal system in Canada, and by interpreting this information to the public, we hope to increase your understanding and appreciation of the importance of the post worldwide and the role it has played in the development of our nation. In this book we examine one large and important chapter in this history: the railway mail service.

For the first time, Canadian mail transportation by train is explored from a social-history perspective. Drawing on archival documents, published reports and the memories of former railway mail clerks, the official *and* unofficial histories of the railway mail service are recounted.

Do you know what happens to your letter after you mail it?

Come aboard and find out what once happened!

Yours sincerely,

Francine Brousseau

Francine Brousseau
Manager, National Postal Museum

Introduction

For more than a century, mail in Canada was carried and processed on board trains. As locomotives steamed their way across the country, postal workers sorted mail in compact post offices aboard railway cars. The first railway post offices operated in 1854; the last in 1971.

Postal workers, organized into crews, spent their working lives crisscrossing the country on train routes. Their shifts began when the train pulled out of the station and ended when the train returned, often several days later. During that time the clerks handled an almost continuous stream of mail removed from bags that were loaded on board, both before the train left the station and at stops along the way. Mail had to be processed quickly in time for it to be dropped off at destinations along the route. Meals were eaten on board and it was not unusual to pass the night on a lumpy bed of mailbags.

Some clerks were assigned to the boats ferrying passengers, supplies and mail to ports along the east and west coasts of Canada and to islands off these coasts. Inside the cramped post-office space provided on these steamers, railway mail clerks sorted mail while their stomachs rolled with the waves. Inevitably, a close cameraderie developed amongst many of these crew members, as well as between them and the train or ship crews. Postal workers were proud to be chosen for the railway mail service as it required more skills than other mail-handling jobs and was suited to those of an adventurous spirit. Twenty years after the demise of the Service, former railway mail clerks across Canada still socialize on a regular basis.

To honour the place of the railway mail service in the history of Canada, and to highlight the achievements of the men whose task it was to sort and bag the mails aboard moving trains, the National Postal Museum chose to mount a special exhibition.

In 1987 research in preparation for the exhibition began. One objective of the exhibition was to humanize the story of the railway mail service, by looking at it

Cramped quarters during the Christmas rush in the London district, 1947

Courtesy of the London Free Press Collection of Photographic Negatives, D.B. Weldon Library, The University of Western Ontario

through the eyes of the postal workers. Consequently, oral history was key to the research plan. Museum staff identified and located surviving former railway mail clerks, many of whom were retired, and some still working for the Post Office, although in new jobs following the dismantling of the railway mail service in 1971. Interviews were conducted with about sixty of these men and their recorded testimonies formed an important basis of information upon which the exhibition was built.

Artifacts relating to the railway mail service were brought together, chosen from the collections of the National Postal Museum, donated by former railway mail clerks, and lent by other public institutions. They were complemented by historical photographs, an audiovisual production, a host of interactive activities and a dramatic exhibit design. **On Track: The Railway Mail Service in Canada** opened to the public in January 1991 at the Canadian Museum of Civilization, and remained there for seven months.

The exhibition was a critical success. Now this book stands as a permanent record of the exhibition, expanding upon the ideas and information presented in it.

Specialized books have been written by philatelists about the postal markings of the railway mail service. These works are of particluar interest to collectors of postal markings who wish to identify items in their collections.

This book, intended for philatelists and general readers alike, is about the operations of the railway mail service, its history, its workers, and its place within the global context of postal communication. Come aboard a railway mail car, meet the people who once processed the mails, and hear some of their stories! You'll trace the route of railway mail, see photographs of the people and objects employed in the railway mail service, and encounter some philatelic postal markings.

Views of the **On Track** *exhibition at the Canadian Museum of Civilization. The design combined postal and railway motifs in an original way.*

Photographs by Claire Dufour

Historical Context

Postal Communication

At the heart of the railway mail service is the idea of communication. Without this basic human need, innovations such as the railway mail service would never have come into being. It is therefore worthwhile to contemplate briefly the communications context in which the postal service, and in turn the railway mail service, existed.

People are social beings. From our earliest prehistoric beginnings, we have congregated into groups. Language developed out of a need for communication between people in these groups. As societies became more complex, their members developed mechanisms to enable long-distance communication. In many instances this took the form of runners who relayed information verbally. With the development of writing, it became possible to send written messages, again carried by runners. In time, formal postal systems were created for government use and, some time later, eventually extended to the general public.

In recent history, wherever people have settled, a system of postal communication has followed. Often this system has been rudimentary—sometimes no more formal than tucking a letter into the pocket of a traveller headed for the same destination as the letter. In the early years of immigration to what we know today as Canada, where there were settlers there was a means of sending and receiving written messages. The implementation of a formal postal system was a priority for the government because, in a large country with a small population, a reliable means of long-distance communication was—and still is—paramount.

Even though the ways of sending and receiving mail have changed over the years, the process of postal communication essentially remains the same. It can be divided into five steps:

1. **Create**: Write a letter, postcard, or other message, produce a magazine, newsletter, catalogue or artwork, package a parcel of goods, and address it.
2. **Send**: Enter the message into the mailstream by depositing it at the post office or into a mail receptacle.
3. **Process**: The Post Office is now entrusted with the message and becomes responsible for routing it so that it will travel with other mail headed for the same destination.
4. **Deliver**: Once the most efficient route has been identified, the message must be transported to its destination.
5. **Receive**: At its destination the message is deposited into a mail receptacle.

A person then opens the letter, magazine, parcel, or other message, and may be prompted to respond by creating and posting a new message. The cycle begins anew.

These five steps form the skeleton of postal communication, but there are many factors that determine how a single message enters and travels through the postal system, and each factor has a different impact on one or more of the steps. For example, the use of trains to transport the mail had the largest impact on the steps involving process and delivery, while the introduction of postage stamps in 1840 mostly affected the sending step. Even though the outward appearance of the postal system changes, the structure is always the same.

Transportation

Most of the milestones in the history of the post are marked by new, more efficient modes of transportation. The postal service cannot exist without transportation, which is clearly the most important factor affecting its appearance. Eras in the history of the post are known by such names as stagecoach mail, steamship mail, pigeon post, balloon post, airmail and railway mail.

No sooner was railway track laid across the vast Canadian landscape during the mid-nineteenth century, then cargoes of mail were carried on board trains. Up until then, the Post Office had relied on horse-drawn vehicles, canoes, or boats for mail transportation, which often took weeks to reach a location.

The building of the railway is credited for the rapid settlement of western Canada during the nineteenth and early twentieth centuries and for the economic expansion of Canada. The railways not only

Loading a "reefer" car full of through mail (mail headed for distant destinations), Saskatoon, Saskatchewan, 1948

Courtesy of the Canadian Postal Archives

stimulated the creation of towns, but brought remote communities out of isolation by linking them with the rest of the country. Trade and industry were stimulated by the railway's efficient means of transporting the rich natural resources of the country to production centres and shipping the finished goods back to consumers. The railway physically linked the disparate regions of the country, making political unification practical. In a very real social, political and economic sense, the railway nurtured the fledgling nation of Canada and encouraged its rise to maturity.

Postal communication was key to people in the new country, both in their personal lives and business affairs. Mail represented the only communication link with the rest of the world. Letters carried news of home, newspapers carried news of the world, packages carried clothing, books, small household items, and even food, while store catalogues contained pictures of articles that could be ordered, paid for, and delivered by post. The first trains to traverse the country carried this mail.

In the history of the railway mail service, trains have sometimes been the only form of transportation used to deliver a piece of mail. Sometimes the train has only had to travel a few miles down the track to deliver the letter to its destination. Often, however, the train has connected with other forms of transportation, such as ship, horse-drawn vehicle, airplane or truck—depending on the time period in history and the location in Canada—to deliver the piece of mail.

Historical Summary

Christmas mail rush, Calgary, Alberta, 1956

Courtesy of the Canadian Postal Archives (POS 2377)

The railway mail service in Canada spans the years 1854 to 1971. However, Post Office involvement with trains began soon after trains were introduced to Canada in 1836, and documents reveal that by 1840, the Post Office was transporting mail by train. As well, although the railway mail service ended in 1971, Canada Post Corporation officially continued to ship mail by train until 1987, though the mail was not processed on board. The peak of the railway mail service occurred in 1950, when more mail was carried by train, more railway mail clerks were employed, and more miles were travelled by railway post offices, than in any other year.

Information for this chapter is drawn from archival documents, particularly from the annual report of the Postmaster General, published each year since 1852.[1] When Britain transferred authority for colonial post offices to the provinces of British North America in 1851, the governments of Canada, consisting of the governments of Canada East (now Quebec), Canada West (now Ontario), Nova Scotia, New Brunswick and Prince Edward Island, assumed responsibility for their respective postal systems and began issuing annual reports. In 1867, when these provinces joined to form Canada, these authorities were consolidated into one. The reports that have been issued every year since by the Canadian Post Office provide a valuable source of information for researchers.

The early reports are particularly useful as they contain a wealth of detailed information, including the names of contractors, employees engaged in the postal service, the routes travelled, as well as a description of disbursements and repairs. These range from leather mailbags to the painting of mailboxes and post office signs, and the purchase of ink, clocks, candles and locks.

Other historical information is gleaned from documents preserved at the National Archives of Canada, custodian of the Canada Post archives since around the turn of the century. Unfortunately, in the years before the National Archives became responsible for these files, they were not saved by the Post Office in any systematic manner. Consequently, many files have been destroyed over the years, and with them, much important historical information has been lost. Drawing on the information that is available, the following chronology presents a digest of some important events in the history of the railway mail service in Canada. Far from being exhaustive, this summary is intended to provide a tableau painted in large brush strokes.

Chronology

1836 The first steam train in Canada makes its inaugural run on the Champlain and St. Lawrence Railroad on July 21. The run extends from La Prairie, just south of Montréal, to St. John's (now called Saint-Jean), a distance of 14.5 miles (23.3 km).[2]

1840 The Post Office Department pays the Champlain and St. Lawrence Railroad fifty-two pounds for the year to transport closed bags of mail by daily coach.[3]

1851 Authority for postal administration is transferred from England to the provinces, and the General Railroad Act is passed. One of its clauses puts all railways under the obligation to carry the mail on demand by the Postmaster General.[4]

1853 The first railway postmark is applied to mail. The earliest known mark was applied on the St. Lawrence and Atlantic Railroad on October 22, 1853.[5] The Postmaster General Report for the year April 1852 to March 1853 states that a postal officer will travel to England to study their system of railroad "travelling post offices" with an eye to adopting this system in Canada.[6] In the meantime, postal conductors accompany the mail on the train, collecting it from station boxes along the way, filled by a messenger from the local post office.[7]

1854 Postal clerks sort mail aboard railway cars specially designed for this purpose. Bags of mail are emptied and their contents sorted inside compact travelling post offices. Disbursements (padlocks and lamps) related to railway post offices are recorded for the first time for the quarter ending March 31, 1854.[8] The first lines in Canada West to employ railway post offices belong to the Great Western Railway (running between Niagara and Hamilton, London and Windsor); the Ontario, Simcoe, and Huron Railway; and the Galt, Brantford, and Buffalo Railway.[9] Contractors are hired to ferry the mail between the rapidly increasing number of train stations and their local post offices. In addition to the mail processed inside these travelling post offices, closed bags of unprocessed mail continue to be shipped by rail.

Partial text of a letter, dated January 26, 1855, written by a railway mail clerk defending himself for missing a mail-train connection owing to a snowstorm.[10] Certainly, the responsibilities of mail clerks were taken very seriously, weather conditions notwithstanding.

Montreal, 26 Jany 1855

Sir,

With reference to my report of yesterday's date, understanding it has been asserted, that the English Mails, which left Pointe Levi on the 21st January, might have arrived in Montreal in time to leave for New York to meet there the Packet Ship for England, I think it my duty to Explain to you more particularly the circumstances which occasioned their detention. —

First. I left Pointe Levi with the said mails on the 21st instant at 9 a.m. The Snow Plough ran off the track four miles below the Chaudière Station. — I enquired how long it would take to get it on to the track. Mr Fosdike, the engineer, told me, that he did not know how long, but that he hoped it would not be very long & that I would get off that night. At 6 P.M. when we came back to Pointe Levi, Mr Webster, the agent there, said: that they were unable to forward the Mails that night, as they had the only Engines required for the Passenger Train next morning. I then represented to him, that it would be better to forward the English Mails & have no Passenger Train next morning: to which he replied: he was very sorry, but that he could not do it, & that moreover

he

1856 The completion of the railway between Québec and Windsor reduces postal delivery time between these cities to about two days, compared with ten-and-a-half days in 1853. The Postmaster General reports:

Great Western Railway

Audit Office   25th December 1854

The Post Master General of Canada
            Dr to the Great Western Railway Company
for conveyance of Mails

Dates		Particulars of Service	Mileage	No of Days	Rate of Pay	Amount		Total	
From	To					$ c	$ c	£ s d	
April 1	December 31	Over Main Line	229	235	$100 per mile, per ann:	17248 39			
August 19	" 31	" Galt Branch	12	115	do do	442 31	17690 70		
	April 9	Special Train			$44 per train	44 00			
	May 14	do			do	44 00			
	October 1	do			do	44 00			
	November 27	do			do	44 00	176 60		
		Totals				17866 70	17866 70	4466 13 6	

An early invoice for the carriage of mails by the Great Western Railway[11]

Besides this gain in speed, further important advantages are reaped in the comparative immunity of Railway Mail conveyance from the irregularities, the damages from exposure to the weather, and other causes of injury unavoidably incidental to the transport of heavy mails by stage or waggon over the ordinary roads of the country, and above all, in the greater security from robbery or loss whilst en route.[12]

1857 The document *General Instructions for Railway Mail Clerks* is drafted, setting forth the clerk's tasks, including the date stamping of all mail passing through his hands. Clerks are told:

> Your duty is one of great responsibility and trust. On its proper performance depends in a great measure the character of the Department for regularity and despatch in the transmission of the Mail.[13]

The Postmaster General reports extensively on the progress of the railway mail service in his annual report for the year ended September 30, 1857:

> On all the more important Railway Lines, the Mails are carried in Post Offices fitted up in a

convenient portion of a Railway Car, and specially appropriated for their reception—and these Railway Post Offices are in charge of Post Office Clerks who travel with the Trains, and assort, distribute, and otherwise prepare the Mails, and collect letters whilst en route to and from the several points on the Line.

This Railway Mail organization is fast assuming the proportions of a separate and most important branch of the Establishment. Already more than 40 Clerks are specially employed in the Railway Post Office service, travelling, each clerk, from 600 to 1,000 miles [960 to 1,600 km] a week in the performance of the above-described duties.

The duties assigned to the Railway Mail Clerks are extremely arduous, and require for their efficient performance a more than usual degree of intelligence and readiness in the persons employed, combined with accurate general knowledge of Post Office duties and regulations, strict integrity and propriety of demeanour, under circumstances which subject these qualifications to unusually severe tests, and physical capability to endure the very considerable bodily fatigue and exposure which naturally attach to the employment.[14]

1859 The completion of the Victoria bridge in Montréal provides an uninterrupted railway link between that city and Portland, Maine. In winter, Canada's transatlantic mails are shipped through the American port, while in summer, steamships carrying mail dock at the city of Québec.[15]

1861 In the ten-year period since 1851, the Post Office in Canada has experienced an explosive growth. The number of letters has increased by 441 per cent, the number of post offices has risen by 295 per cent, and postal revenue is up by 297 per cent.[16]

1863 The Railway Postal Service Act is passed. It acknowledges the importance of an efficient postal system by authorizing the Postmaster General to demand any railway company to carry mail, according to a schedule convenient to the operations of the Post Office, and to construct post offices inside railway cars, complete with heat and light. The Post Office will pay a mileage

POST OFFICE DEPARTMENT

Québec, 22nd March 1861

Sir,

With reference to the accommodation provided by the Grand Trunk Railway for the British Mails during their weekly transmission from Montréal and Québec to Portland; I have the honor to report that, on my arrival at Richmond on the morning of Saturday the 15th inst with the Québec portion of the mails for the United Kingdom for dispatch by the Steamship "Norwegian", I found the Montréal portion of the mails in question in an ordinary Baggage Car, the doors of which there was no means of fastening, and through which, the employees of the Railway were continually passing. There was no light provided for the Officer in charge, and the small stove at the further end of the car from where the mail were (sic) placed, afforded no protection whatever against the inclemency of the weather.

After removing the mail twice to shelter them (sic) in some measure from the snow which drifted through every door in the car, I was compelled, in order to escape from the intensity of the cold, to have the mails removed into the sleeping car on Sunday morning the 16th inst, in which car they remained till my arrival in Portland on Monday morning....

Partial text of Post Office inspector's report to the Postmaster General on the operations of the railway post office running between Québec and Portland, Maine, March 22, 1861[17]

rate according to a schedule of services provided. Uncooperative railway companies will be fined a penalty.[18] This bill was a response to Post Office complaints that railway companies showed indifference to the mail and treated its transmission more as a favour than a duty, in contravention of the Post Office clause of the *General Railroad Act of 1851.*[19]

1865 Following a decade-long dispute between the Post Office and railway companies, a judicial commission rules on the rates of compensation to be paid for the conveyance of mail for the years 1858 to 1868. Because of this disagreement, companies such as the Great Western Railway had threatened several times to withdraw services during the 1850s. Specifically, they sought compensation for the extra costs incurred by running night trains in order to meet mail delivery schedules, making extra station stops to unload mail, fitting up post offices inside baggage cars, and hiring extra staff to guard the mail. An Order-in-Council fixed subsidy rates in 1858, but the Grand Trunk Railway rejected them, leading to the creation of an arbitration board six years later to settle the dispute.

In 1863, the Grand Trunk Railway announced service cutbacks on trains connecting with the ocean mail until such time as payment was received. This action underscored the growing importance of the railways to postal communication, not only within British North America, but also between the colonies and the rest of the world by virtue of the railway connection with Portland, Maine, where ocean mail steamers docked in winter. The Great Western Railway, too, expounded on its vital role in mail transportation in a thirty-one-page treatise submitted to the Post Office in 1863.[20]

1867 Upon Confederation, the Post Office of the Dominion of Canada is created, uniting the postal systems of Prince Edward Island, Nova Scotia, New Brunswick, Quebec and Ontario under one department. The Act took effect April 1, 1868. Work progresses on extending the railway mail service network throughout the Maritime provinces.[21]

1875 Mail begins to be carried by the Prince Edward Island Railway.[22]

1876 The Intercolonial Railway is completed, linking the Maritime and central Canada rail systems and reducing by about twelve hours the time taken to deliver mail from Halifax or Saint John to Ontario. Every weekday there are sixty-four railway post offices in operation on 4,486 miles (7,177.6 km) of track.[23]

1883 Thirteen years after entering Confederation, Manitoba residents begin to receive mail by trains that follow an all-Canadian route, no longer passing over American soil. The Canadian Pacific Railway is completed through to Calgary.[24]

1885 Along the Canadian Pacific Railway under construction in British Columbia, a rudimentary
post office is established on the supply train for
the convenience of the construction workers
("navvies"). As the laying of track advances
westward, so does the post office. Postmarking
its mail "End of Track," the post office operates
from January 1 to November 7, 1885, when the
track of the eastward crew meets up with the
track of the westward crew at Craigellachie to
produce an unbroken transcontinental railway.
During the ten months that it operated, the End
of Track post office issued almost as many money
orders as the major Québec post office.[25]

*This photograph provides one
of the earliest glimpses of a
railway mail car, circa 1885,
Canadian Pacific Railway.*

*Courtesy of the Canadian Postal
Archives (POS 2387)*

1886 With the completion of the Canadian Pacific
Railway, daily mail car service begins between
the Atlantic and Pacific oceans, spanning 3,740
miles (5,984 km). The first through passenger
train leaves Montréal on June 28 and arrives
in Port Moody, British Columbia, six days
later. The number of railway mail clerks is now
304, up from 137 in 1873. The Postmaster
General reports:

> The Railway Mail Clerks travelling in charge of
> these Postal cars receive and distribute

The first train to travel from Montréal to the Pacific Coast, 1886

Courtesy of the National Archives of Canada (PA 66579)

correspondence daily over the whole line from Halifax to the Pacific Coast, and correspondence passes between the Postal cars on the several sections into which the railways forming the line are divided for working purposes without suffering detention at any intermediate point.[26]

1889 The hand-to-hand system of registered mail begins. Railway mail clerks now begin and end their shifts at the post office where they pick up and deliver registered mail.[27]

1897 The Post Office Department creates the Railway Mail Service Branch to administer this increasingly expansive transportation sector that now dominates other forms of mail transportation. The distance travelled by railway mail clerks amounts to 9,120,761 miles (14,593,217 km) in fiscal year 1896-97, while mailbags travel 5,997,765 miles (9,596,424 km) in baggage cars.[28] This growth is consistent with the rapid expansion of the

Railway mail clerks dressed as seamen when they were assigned to ships carrying mail to the outports of Newfoundland. The cotton mailbag bears the markings of the Newfoundland Post Office, which was independent until 1949, when Newfoundland joined Canada.

National Postal Museum 1989.27.3,.4 (uniform and identification card)

Gift of George Ledrew, Mount Pearl, Newfoundland (St. John's district, 1955-1968)

National Postal Museum 1990.14.5 (mailbag)

Gift of Edgar Skanes, St. John's, Newfoundland (St. John's district, 1946-1968)

Photograph by Claire Dufour

railway network in Canada during the late nineteenth century, evident in the construction of two more transcontinental railways to handle traffic. The railway mail service is divided into nine geographic districts, each headed by a superintendent. An Act sets the salary scale and terms of employment of railway mail clerks.

1897 In Newfoundland, the completion of the railway permits the carriage of mail between St. John's and Port aux Basques, where it is shipped by mail steamer to North Sydney, Nova Scotia, and is then moved by railway to mainland destinations. Railway mail clerks run the post office on these ships and on the coastal steamers that ply the waters off Newfoundland and Labrador. In the British tradition, these post offices are called travelling post offices.

The Royal Mail truck transports mail and passengers from Ottawa station in December, 1909, where the first Canadian Northern Railway train has just arrived.

Courtesy of the National Archives of Canada (PA 165400)

1901 Mail travels north by train to Whitehorse in the Yukon Territory.[29]

1913 There are now more than one thousand employees in the Railway Mail Service Branch (compared to 385 in 1897). Railway mail clerks travel the thousands of miles of track laid in the West during the last five years on lines owned chiefly by the Grand Trunk Pacific, Canadian Northern and Canadian Pacific railways.[30]

1914 A new fee schedule is set, generously increasing the remuneration paid by the Post Office to railway companies.[31]

1917 The Dominion Railway Mail Clerks' Federation is created, uniting the various regional associations that began as early as 1889. The Federation is not a union, so members have no bargaining power and cannot strike.[32]

1918 The first official airmail flight takes place, flying from Montréal to Toronto. Over the next few decades, this mode of delivery will have a profound effect on the railway mail service.

1921 City sorting begins on non-stop runs between Montréal and Toronto. The volume of mail is so great between these two centres that clerks sort mail only for the city at the other end of the line, rather than for stops along the way. The mail is sorted by letter-carrier route. Upon arrival at the terminal, the mail is ready to be delivered.

Following the report of the Board of Railway Commissioners tabled in Parliament in 1919, the Post Office's allotment for railway transportation effectively doubles to eight million dollars per year.[33]

1929 Railway mail clerks are now compensated for their increased responsibilities relative to other mail handlers. Clerks are graded according to their level of seniority and the complexity of their run, and remuneration is tied to this grade. Their mileage allowance is also graded. This system results in higher pay for railway mail clerks, particularly those travelling long distances on the main lines.[34]

1939 King George VI and Queen Elizabeth tour Canada, marking the first visit by a reigning monarch in Canada's history. The Royal party crosses the country by train and a railway post office accompanies the train to process the Royal mail. (See the chapter on *The Royal Train*.)

1944 The Dominion Railway Mail Clerks' Federation affiliates with the Civil Service Federation, and in later years with other labour congresses.

1948 The Post Office introduces "All-Up" service. By this policy, all domestic first-class mail is carried by plane at regular postage rates.

Airplanes begin to offer a serious challenge to trains for mail transportation, Manitoba, 1938.

Courtesy of the National Archives of Canada (PA 130761)

Royal Mail trucks are dedicated to Post Office transportation needs, Calgary, circa 1958.

Courtesy of the Canadian Postal Archives (POS 2363)

Trains carry only the lesser classes of mail, as well as first-class mail headed for places not accessible by plane.

1950 The railway mail service reaches its peak in size and scope. Here are some statistics:[35]

Railway post offices..192
Baggage cars (containing closed bags of mail)........834
Railway mail clerks...1,385
Miles travelled by railway post offices.......22,489,547
(35,983,275 km)
Miles travelled by railway mail clerks.......59,227,907
(94,764,651 km)
Steamboat (domestic) routes where mail is sorted.....85

A national railway strike during the summer gives trucking companies a foothold in carrying mail. The quality of roads and the reliability of motor vehicles has improved to the point that "motor transport is finding an increasingly important place in the transportation of mail."[36] More and more people prefer cars to trains for long-distance travel.

With the consequent reduction in passenger train schedules, mail delivery suffers. Post Office officials realize that long-haul trucks are not restricted by set schedules, but can

For one hundred years, the railway mail service network corresponded to that of the railways: wherever railway track was laid, mail trains travelled. Then in the two decades following 1951, the railway mail service shrank away to nothing.

Bidding farewell to the Moose Jaw-Calgary railway post office, June 23, 1965

Courtesy of the Canadian Postal Archives (POS 2388)

leave at any time of day or night, in almost any weather, entirely at the convenience of their client, the Post Office. Additionally, the dramatic increase in mail correspondence caused by the post-war population and economic boom is taxing the ability of railway post offices to handle it all.

1951 Air Parcel Post is introduced, further loosening the grip of trains on mail transportation.[37]

1961 A decade following the heyday of the railway mail service, the number of railway post offices has been reduced by two thirds to sixty-five, and the number of clerks is reduced by more than half to 647.[38]

1965 Railway post offices cease to operate west of Winnipeg. This is precipitated by the decision of Canadian Pacific Railway to withdraw mail-carrying facilities on its trans-Canada routes.[39] Bulk mail continues to be carried on express freight trains.

1966 Between 1957 and 1966, the number of postal employees has increased from 30,000 to 44,000, and mail volume has risen to 4.9 billion pieces.[40] The Post Office begins experimenting with automated mail-processing machinery, leading to the implementation of the postal code in 1971 and a new distribution network based on the highways and airports of the nation.

The Dominion Railway Mail Clerks' Association is dissolved when its members join the principal union of the federal civil service, the Public Service Alliance of Canada. For the first time, railway mail clerks can negotiate a contract with their employer. There are now only twenty-six railway post offices in operation, employing 330 clerks.[41]

1968 The last mail car runs in Newfoundland.

1971 The railway mail service ends officially on April 24. Crews process mail for the last time on the five remaining runs: Lévis-Campbellton, Campbellton-Lévis, Ottawa-Toronto, Toronto-Ottawa, and Montréal-Toronto. (On February 2, the last mail car runs from eastern Canada to Winnipeg, and on January 31 the last mail car in the Maritimes runs between Halifax and Campbellton.) An official ceremony covered by the press is held at Lévis, Quebec, when the very last train pulls into station on April 24. Dignitaries from the Post Office and Canadian National Railway make speeches to commemorate the passing of this historic era. The Post Office continues to transport bulk mail by train, stored in sealed containers.

1973 A railway mail car is brought out of storage to process mail generated by the Royal party of Queen Elizabeth II and the accompanying press who travelled by Royal train during her visit to Canada.

1987 Canada Post Corporation officially switches from trains to trucks for the bulk shipping of overland mail.

A sombre scene on the Campellton-Lévis last run, April 24, 1971

Courtesy of the Canadian Postal Archives (POS 2239) and Canada Post
Corporation

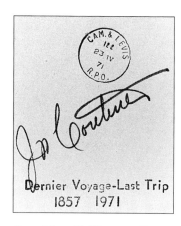

Jean-Marc Taillon, a railway mail clerk in the Québec district from 1948 to 1961, collected a souvenir facing slip signed by crew member J.N. Couturier on the last Campbellton-Lévis run.

Gift of Jean-Marc Taillon

National Postal Museum 1988.55.7

Photograph by Steve Darby

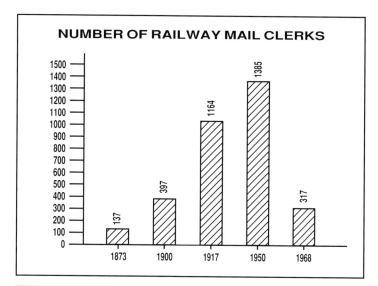

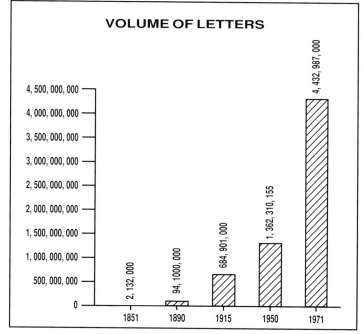

These two charts compare the number of railway mail clerks to the climbing volume of letter mail over a century. Railway mail cars could not handle the huge leap in mail volume that took place during the mid-twentieth century.

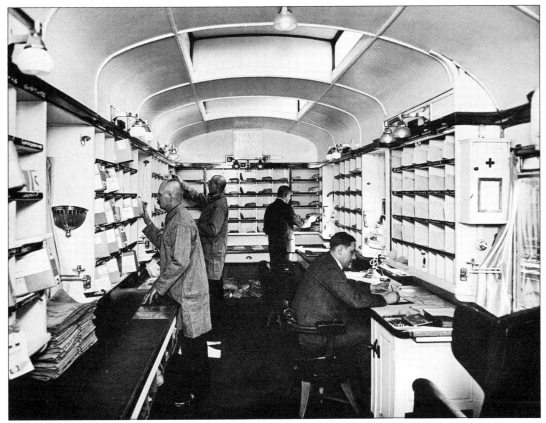

Foreign Context

The railway mail service thrives to this day in many countries around the world. Particularly in Europe, where distances are short and passenger-train traffic heavy, railway mail cars make economic sense.

The National Postal Museum sent out a questionnaire in 1989, to which the following countries answered that they still operate a railway mail service:

Interior and exterior views of a modern mail car in Hungary

Courtesy of the Postamúzeum, Budapest, Hungary

- Austria
- China
- Czechoslovakia (The Czech and Slovak Federal Republic)
- Finland
- France
- Germany
- Hungary
- Italy
- Luxembourg
- Norway
- Poland
- Portugal
- Spain
- Sweden
- Switzerland
- Turkey
- U.S.S.R. (now the Commonwealth of Independent States)

403

CANADIAN   PACIFIC

212   COACH

CANADIAN

MAII   3456

C.P.R.

ANADIAN   PACIFIC

3075   BA

Railway Mail Operations

Creating the Message

The first step in the postal communication process is the creation of a message. The kinds of messages—letters, postcards, catalogues, parcels, newspapers, magazines—and their volume, can provide an insight into the activities of Canadians during the days of the railway mail service. The *raison d'être* of the railway mail service was to deliver the mail, but what kinds of mail did it handle?

NEWSPAPERS

Readers in rural areas and small towns have long depended upon the post for news of the world, particularly in the days before television. Through an efficient network of train routes and connections, most readers could receive their city newspapers by post the day after printing. So important was the timely arrival of the newspaper, the Post Office gave it priority treatment.

Wilbrod Ross (Québec district, 1946-1971) remembers the large volume of newspapers he handled each day on the Campbellton-Gaspé run. He and his fellow workers handled newspapers right after the registered and first-class mail was sorted, putting the newspapers with the first-class mail or into special bags marked "Newspaper." Printed in Québec the evening before, *Le Soleil* could be delivered by rail to a reader along the lower Saint Lawrence River by lunchtime.[42]

Good shot! Andy Smyth on the Ottawa-Toronto run sorts the newspaper into the correct bag, circa 1948.

Courtesy of the National Archives of Canada (PA 122580)

MAIL ORDER CATALOGUES

Former postmasters have estimated that during the first half of the twentieth century, the ratio of parcel mail to first-class mail averaged ten to one.[43] Former railway mail clerks add that there was a surge in parcel mail during December and August. The December surge corresponds, of course, to Christmas gift exchanges, and in late summer parents placed orders for children's clothing and supplies in preparation for the new school year.

This huge volume of parcel mail attests to an important fact in the history of our country: from the late 1800s to the 1950s, rural Canada shopped by mail. Prior to the urbanization of Canada and the onset of travel by private motor vehicle, rural and small-town inhabitants ordered and received their manufactured goods through the mail. Department stores such as Eaton's, Simpsons and the Army and Navy Store operated massive mail-order units to handle the receipt and dispatch of orders.

R. Boyd of Carlsbad Springs, Ontario, ordered his garden seeds by catalogue during the 1940s.

National Postal Museum

Photograph by Steve Darby

At that time you have to remember that the whole economy, the whole way business was done in the small villages, it was all Eaton's and Simpsons; they had catalogues and everyone bought everything from them. There was no clothing store, no...baker...so everything was brought in from Eaton's and Simpsons. That meant big business for the post office, you understand: everything, absolutely everything, came from Toronto.

(Paul-Émile Bourassa, Montréal district, 1946-1971)

Such was the efficiency of both the postal system and the mail-order departments, that it was quite normal for a consumer to receive merchandise within the same week of sending in an order. Robert Strachan (Winnipeg district, 1946-1966) remembers seeing the Eaton's truck waiting for the train at the Winnipeg terminal. No sooner were the bags for Eaton's unloaded, than the truck was whisking the bounty of orders off to the warehouse for processing. In 1914 the Post Office responded to the burgeoning demand for mail-order goods by increasing the weight limit on parcel post to eleven pounds (5.2 kg).

GREETING CARDS

Each year, the contents of first-class mailbags balloon during the months of February and December as Canadians continue a long-standing tradition of exchanging greetings. Valentine and Christmas cards, respectively, clog the postal system.

> I remember one of the worst trips I ever made to Montréal was a Friday night out of Toronto, Friday the 13th and I don't remember what year it was but they still had letter-carrier delivery on Saturday. And of course Valentine's Day being the next day, the 14th, I started sorting letters in the station of Toronto at about 9:30 at night and I was still sorting—I sorted without a break—I was still sorting letters in the station of Brockville at 5:30 the next morning.
>
> *(Michael Millar, Toronto district, 1965-1971)*

These dainty Valentine cards date from the late nineteenth century.

*National Postal Museum
1983. 192.53, .100, .108*

Photograph by Steve Darby

LIVE SPECIMENS

In 1922, the Post Office decided to permit the transportation of day-old chicks by mail. The high-pitched chirps of baby chicks and the low hum of buzzing bees were commonplace sounds inside the mail car for it was, and still is, typical for farmers to ship chicks and bees by mail. Many a story is told of bees escaping from their shipping crates but, fortunately for railway mail clerks, these escapees were more interested in swarming close to the queen bee than to human beings. Mail delivery had to be fast; if not, the chicks would die.

Cartoonist Harry Hall, who began working in the railway mail service in the Moose Jaw, Saskatchewan, district in 1914, satirizes the Post Office's decision to allow day-old chicks to be carried by mail.

Courtesy of the Canadian Postal Archives

Copy for Book.

24365

POST OFFICE DEPARTMENT, CANADA.

CIRCULAR NO. 1063

5.21

Postal Service Branch,

Railway Mail Service,

Ottawa, February 6, 1925.

Transmission of Day Old Chicks
Parcel Post.

Attention is directed to January Supplement of Postal Guide, page 6, clause 3, and in connection therewith the following additional instructions appear advisable.

Care must be exercised in handling day old chicks in postal cars to guard against extremes of heat and cold. Containers should not be placed too close to steam coils.

Shipments that have been inadvertently accepted by and despatched from Post Offices where delivery must be effected through Baggage Car Service, via Catch Post Service or lengthy Water Service, when received by a Railway Mail Clerk must be at once returned to said office by most expeditious despatch.

Railway Mail Clerks should be instructed to report all cases of receipt of shipments that require more than thirty-six hours in transit. Such report will indicate name and address of shipper and addressee. This is particularly desirable in connection with matter originating in United States. Full particulars of such reports are to be transmitted to this service for suitable action.

It is advisable that records be kept of quantity of this class of matter so that the District Office may be in a position at end of mailing period, to give fairly detailed information similar to that required in questionnaire 1020-A-19-12-'24.

Chief Superintendent of the
Railway Mail Service.

The District Superintendent
of Postal Service,

FOOD

Food was also shipped by mail. Eggs were particularly commonplace, but of course, other foods were transported as well—some of them legally, some of them not so legally. In addition to their many other duties, railway mail clerks had to be on the lookout for such restricted items as whisky bottles.

> People used to send whisky through the mail. They put it into a hollowed-out loaf of bread. In that time you didn't have sliced bread, they hollowed the bread and at Christmastime they stuck a bottle of whisky in a hollow loaf of bread and sent it in a parcel and you had to try to catch that and see that it was turned over to the RCMP.
>
> *(Donald McCarthy, Ottawa district, 1958-1971)*

So commonplace was it for eggs and other perishables to be transported by mail that special mailing labels were created.

National Postal Museum 1990.34.15, 1990.34.22

Photograph by Steve Darby

Sending eggs by mail at an urban post office, 1923

Courtesy of the National Archives of Canada (PA 61544)

BALLOT BOXES

The presence of fifty galvanized steel boxes with sharp, unforgiving corners crammed into the end of the mail car was a sure sign of a government election. Special mailing labels attached to the boxes indicated their destination.

Railway mail clerks dreaded election time. Ballot boxes were large and cumbersome, and thousands of them were all shipped at once, just before and just after an election.

We used to get those things after an election and they were...a nuisance because of course they were sent back registered mail to the chief of the electoral office in Ottawa. And after an election we would get these things—and of course they take fabulous space—and you get into a place like Kingston and they might come up with fifty or sixty or more ballot boxes and of course you have to stack these things as best you could in the corner of the mail car.

(Michael Millar, Toronto district, 1965-1971)

Ballot box courtesy of Elections Canada

Mailing label courtesy of Brian Murphy, Ottawa, Ontario

Photographs by Steve Darby

Cotton money bags were a common sight on board mail cars.

Courtesy of the Bank of Montreal Archives

Photograph by Steve Darby

CURRENCY AND GOLD

If ever the trade of the railway mail clerk was dangerous, it was because the bank notes, coins and gold they often carried were an easy target for professional thieves. Armed with nothing more than a cancelling hammer to protect themselves and their cargo, mail clerks were put in charge of the safe passage of huge amounts of money or gold.

Trains travelling from mines in the north to urban centres in the south carried gold nuggets or ingots, while cash for the payroll travelled north by return train. Mutilated bills were sent from banks back to the Royal Canadian Mint. In Nova Scotia, in one memorable heist, a thief locked a crew of mail clerks into a tiny one-person bathroom while he made his escape. Clarence Tobin (Halifax district, 1944-1967) reports that the men were on the verge of suffocation when they were discovered hours later.

Post Office Department, Canada

5.20

OFFICE OF THE

GENERAL SUPERINTENDENT OF POSTAL SERVICE

25160

Ottawa, June 22nd, 1928.

Copy for the BOOK

Confidential

Circular No. 1178.

All District Superintendents and
        P.O.Inspector, Charlottetown.

Dear Sir,-   Safe-guarding Mails.

        The circumstances surrounding the mail
robbery at Toronto Tuesday night indicates the necessity
for providing additional safeguards to valuable mail other
than usual precautions covered by previous general instructions issued in Circular 853, 28th February 1922, and 1148,
1st October 1926.

        You will be good enough, therefore, to
instruct Railway Mail Clerks of your District that all doors
of postal cars are to be kept locked at all times, except
when mail is being taken in at the doors.

        This will necessitate any one, not actually
at work in the car, knocking for admission and will enable
the Clerk answering the door to establish identity before
permitting access to car, and should preclude the possibility
of a surprise attack.

                    Yours very truly,

                        General Superintendent of
                            Postal Service.

A 1928 circular warns railway mail clerks to be vigilant against thieves.
Courtesy of the National Archives of Canada[45]

Waiting for the train, station letter box in background, circa 1900

Courtesy of the Canadian Postal Archives (POS 2369)

Sending the Message

Letter boxes have now been placed at all the principal stations on the leading railways in the Dominion, in which prepaid letters may be posted without additional charge. The letters posted in these letter boxes are, for the most part, collected by the railway mail clerks on duty in the post office cars upon the several railways; in a few places, where the trains do not stop long enough to admit of the clerks leaving the cars, the collection is made by couriers who hand the letters to

OPPOSITE PAGE:

This station letter box, made of cast iron, dates from the late nineteenth century and bears the coat of arms used during the reign of Queen Victoria. The "lion's paw" or "beaver tail" clasp lifts to expose the padlock securing the mail inside. The time of the next mail pick up is displayed in a small window on the side of the box After collecting the mail, the clerk turns a dial inside the box to display the next collection time.

National Postal Museum 1985.160

Photograph by Claire Dufour

the mail clerks in the travelling post offices. The accommmodation thus afforded enables the public to post letters and postcards up to the last moment without extra charge, and is found to be a great convenience to persons travelling.

(Report of the Postmaster General, 1890)[46]

The distinctive red mailbox is a familiar symbol of the Canadian post office. Mounted onto telephone poles or placed on sidewalks, the mailbox is the most recognizable and ubiquitous face of the Post Office.

Once the correspondence has been written, the envelope or wrapper addressed, and the postage affixed, the piece of mail is ready for posting. The mailbox is where the sender and Post Office first connect; the point at which the sender entrusts custody of a piece of mail to the postal system.

Mail receptacles come in an assortment of shapes, sizes and colours. In addition to railway station boxes, there are street boxes, boxes inside post offices, drop chutes in the walls of post offices, hotel lobby boxes, and at the foot of rural driveways there are often private mailboxes, which serve to both dispatch and receive mail.

This chapter presents some examples of mail receptacles, all dating from the days of the railway mail service, and some of them unique to the Service. They all mark the point where a piece of mail enters the mail stream.

This post office wicket from Peterborough, Ontario, was built by the Office Specialty Company (Toronto) around 1920. Mail is deposited through the brass mail slot beneath the window where the postmaster sells postage stamps and money orders. A bank of post office boxes would have flanked the wicket.

National Postal Museum
1974.2183

Photograph by Claire Dufour

Metal "transit boxes" provided a unique way of posting letters on trains without a post office. Located in the baggage car, the box was used by passengers or by townspeople at station stops. The box remained locked until the end of the run, when it was taken to the local post office to be emptied by the postmaster. This box was used between Nakina and Armstrong in northern Ontario on the Canadian National Railway line during the mid-twentieth century.

National Postal Museum 1987.67.3

Photograph by Claire Dufour

Every railway mail car had a slot in the side of the car for the receipt of mail. While the train idled in the station, townspeople could post their letters directly into the mail car for immediate handling by the mail clerks. This photograph depicts a modern mail car in Italy, where the railway mail service still operates today.

Courtesy of the Amministrazione delle Poste e delle Telecomunicazioni, Italy (Detail)

The first mailboxes in Canada appeared on the streets of downtown Toronto in 1859. These free-standing, pillar-style boxes were replaced around 1880 by the post-mounted style of box shown here.

National Postal Museum 1974.864.1

Photograph by Claire Dufour

Toronto, 1920. Concerned with getting their newspapers to subscribers quickly, publishers assisted the Post Office by pre-sorting, bagging, and delivering the newspapers directly to the train. The Post Office offered a reduced postage rate to large-volume mailers who facilitated the work of postal handlers in this way.

Courtesy of the National Archives of Canada (PA 59949)

From the outside, mail cars could be distinguished from passenger or freight cars by their window and door configuration. These model train cars were built by James O'Connor, a former railway mail clerk.

National Postal Museum
1974.2090.1

Photograph by Claire Dufour

Processing and Delivering the Message

Step aboard a postal car to view the physical heart of the railway mail service, and listen to former railway mail clerks describe their work in these travelling post offices. The memories of about sixty former railway mail clerks were tapped for their recollections of the unofficial history of the railway mail service and for details on the day-to-day operations of the postal cars, when they were interviewed for the National Postal Museum in 1987.[47]

While most of the clerks had begun their work in the 1940s, some old-timers could remember back to the 1930s or 1920s and, in one exceptional case, the clerk had begun his days "on the road" in 1913! (The names of railway mail clerks who were interviewed are listed in the Appendix.)

So vivid are the memories of these men and so colourful are the tableaux they painted of their days "on the road," that their own words have been used to invoke the spirit of the time and place. Notice how the self-described comportment of the clerks does not always correspond to that prescribed by the Post Office in the printed circulars distributed to them regularly!

The tasks undertaken by railway mail clerks fall broadly into four categories: sorting the mail (including loading and unloading mailbags); cancelling the mail; filling out forms; and operating the catchpost. Each of these activities, as they took place circa 1950, is described in a section of this chapter.

APPEARANCE OF THE MAIL CAR

Generally speaking, the mail-handling activities inside a mail car duplicated those of a conventional post office. The primary difference was that railway mail clerks did not provide over-the-counter services. They did not sell postage stamps, money orders, registered, special delivery or insurance services; did not operate a Post Office Savings Bank branch; and did not hold mail for customer pick-up, just to name a few of the services provided by conventional post offices.

The interior of a mail car resembled a compact version of the mail-handling area of a regular post office, except the furnishings were adapted to withstand the lurches and jolts of a speeding vehicle.

Railway post offices came in various sizes. On the main railway lines that connected the major cities of the nation, the post office could occupy the entire length of a twenty-two metre (seventy-two-foot) car, and up to ten clerks would be needed to handle the huge volume of mail. A more typical length of mail car was eighteen metres (sixty feet), staffed by about five men.

On the secondary "branch" lines running off the main lines, regional mail was easily accommodated in a nine-metre long (thirty-foot), three-man post office. Baggage occupied the other half of the eighteen-metre long car. "Overflow" mailbags that didn't fit inside the mail car were stored inside the baggage compartment and moved from one

section to another as it became their turn to be processed. The smallest railway post offices, which
handled local mail on small branch lines, measured
four-and-a-half claustrophobic metres (fifteen feet)
in length and were manned by one lonely clerk. The
rest of this "budd car" held baggage.

In 1868, specifications for the construction of mail
cars called for a corridor to run along one side, leaving room for only a long, narrow post office.
Squeezed into this tiny space were letter-sorting
cases, newspaper-sorting cases, special drawers for
registered mail and a counter. Wicker baskets provided an alternative to mailbags.[48]

Regardless of size, every railway post office was
equipped with a cantilevered "dumping" table, sorting cases, bag racks, sorting "cages" above the bag
racks, and stanchions (to support the stacks of mailbags), all secured firmly to the car infrastructure. As
well, each car was furnished with a toilet, sink and
stove for the convenience of the clerks. In the days of

*Posing inside a mail car, circa
1905. Mail cars were staffed
by a crew of one to ten clerks,
depending on the size of post
office and the volume of mail
on board. The layout varies
little from a postal car sixty
years later, though the
construction of the car itself
changed from wood to steel.*

*Courtesy of the National Archives
of Canada (PA 59920)*

Make up your mail for the first office at which you arrive, enclose it in a Leather Bag which [sic] label, secure carefully with a lock and deliver at the appointed Station. (General Instructions for Railway Mail Clerks, 1857[50]) *Until 1920, leather mailbags were used in the mail service. Their heavy brass locks secured the registered and first-class mail within.*

National Postal Museum
1974.506

Photographs by Claire Dufour

steam power, mail cars were often heated by a coal-burning, pot-bellied stove. As one former railway mail clerk, A.J. Janssens, has described, mail cars were "...a marvel of compactness, embodying in a limited space all necessary working, storage, toilet and cooking facilities."[49]

In order to accommodate men and mail, the bag racks could be folded up against the wall when not in use, the reversible dumping table flipped to either side of its central post, and even the sink folded against the wall to make more room in the tiny bathroom.

A late-nineteenth century railway mail clerk would be quite at home in a mid-twentieth century mail car.

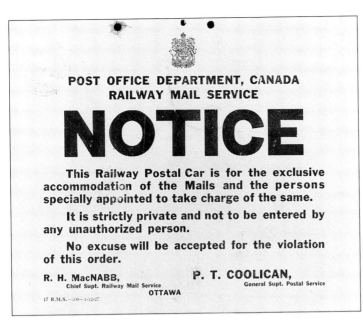

POST OFFICE DEPARTMENT, CANADA
RAILWAY MAIL SERVICE

NOTICE

This Railway Postal Car is for the exclusive accommodation of the Mails and the persons specially appointed to take charge of the same.

It is strictly private and not to be entered by any unauthorized person.

No excuse will be accepted for the violation of this order.

R. H. MacNABB,
Chief Supt. Railway Mail Service

P. T. COOLICAN,
General Supt. Postal Service

OTTAWA

17 R.M.S.—500—1-12-27.

Once a piece of mail enters the postal system, the Post Office becomes responsible for its security. Postal-sorting areas are therefore limited to authorized personnel. This sign, dated 1927, was posted in mail cars.

National Postal Museum
1990.34.3

Photograph by Steve Darby

Operations remained essentially the same over the years, as did the furnishings and materials.

The most significant change occurred when, during the early twentieth century, diesel power replaced steam. This had a significant impact on the clerk, forcing him to work at a much greater speed. In the days of steam, frequent stops to take on coal and water reduced the overall speed of the train, buying time for the clerk as he struggled to finish sorting the mail for the next drop-off. The increase in speed achieved by diesel power, however, forced clerks to sort the mail more rapidly in order to have the bags ready for their drop-off points.

Although the faster speed dictated faster work, at least the diesel-powered ride was smoother and the electric lighting brighter and more constant than on steam trains, making the clerks' reading task easier than it had been when lights were powered by gas or batteries. The electric heat of diesel trains was more reliable than steam heat, but diesel fumes were noxious. And while the pace of work was speedier during the days of diesel, the clerks benefitted from a shorter week than their early twentieth-century colleagues had worked, thanks to interventions on their behalf by the Dominion Railway Mail Clerks' Association.

Tools and materials for sorting mail include twine, twine cutters (scissors, finger knives), "header" labels and facing slips. During the mid-twentieth century, elastic bands replaced twine for bundling sorted letters together, a gesture of economy since elastic bands could be reused several times. (Previously, mail clerks had been instructed to cut the twine on letter bundles as close to the knot as possible in order to reuse it.)

National Postal Museum
1974.434.1, 1974.1071.17,
1974.1379.1, 1987.41.1f,
1990.20.1

Photograph by Claire Dufour

SORTING THE MAIL

Mail sorting accounted for the lion's share of the railway mail clerk's work. It was, and still is, the heart of all mail operations. Bags of mail, ranging in number from one to two hundred, were loaded on board and stacked from floor to ceiling inside the mail car or heaved into a baggage compartment. As soon as they were loaded, the task of emptying and sorting their contents began. Not all mail was handled directly by the clerks. "Through" mail simply hitched a ride to get to the other side of a district on its way to distant destinations.

> The mail courier comes to the door and gives you the mail and you give him a bag for his bag. You take his bag and dump it on the sorting table in the middle of the mail car and sort this bundle into different bags, which are labelled with different cities, and then the one for the next stop you pack up and throw off when the train stops.
>
> *(Harold T. Elgie, London district, 1942-1964)*

Beginning with registered and first-class mail, the clerk dumped the contents of a bag onto the central table (variously called a "facing", "sorting", "dumping" or "Kendal" table), grabbed a handful of letters, "faced" them right side up so the addresses could be read, and commenced sorting. All letters for a common destination were put into the same slot (pigeon hole). Once full, the contents of each pigeon hole were removed, tied into a bundle, labelled with a facing slip marked with the destination, and dropped into a bag with other mail headed for the same destination.

> Then you get on the mail car and the first thing we do is what we call label up the racks and the boxes that were above us, then we start sorting what we call the locks in the lock bags where the first-class mail and the registers are, and after that we start sorting parcel mail....The mail was piled in the back in what we called the stanchions....The mail that was for points along the line we sorted that first, and other areas of B.C. we sorted that afterwards.
>
> *(Norman Johnston, Calgary district, 1948-1965)*

If the distance between sender and receiver was great, the first sortation would likely take the letter to an interim destination where it would be loaded onto a different train or other form of transportation. If transferred to a new train, the letter could be sorted all over again and directed to a new destination. Each of these handlings brought the letter closer to its final address.

To sort mail, railway mail clerks had to know the locations of thousands of post offices and their connecting routes. The very effectiveness of the postal system depended upon their ability in this regard. It was essential that the clerks keep abreast of changes in train (and steamer) routes and schedules—and in later years, airplane and truck schedules—to move the mail efficiently. (More is said about this in the chapter on *Life on Board.*)

Certainly, the routing of a letter might be as direct as two train whistles down the line. However, cross-country mail addressed to out-of-the-way destinations could involve a zigzag pattern of train routes, as well as other forms of transportation.

Every seven to eight minutes there was a station, so every seven to eight minutes we had a bag to close, even if our way mail wasn't finished, we handed over what was ready; the rest we delivered coming back next morning.

(Paul Émile Jobin, Québec district, 1954-1963)

After six hours of sorting I would still be doing forty-six letters a minute. I wasn't one of the fastest: there was a guy named Charlie Shaw in Toronto...Charlie Shaw, you know, I think he sorted fifty-four letters or something a minute; you had to do it damned fast, you understand. Naturally you couldn't go that fast with everything, but, you know, typed letters and business letters could be sorted pretty quickly.

(Irénée Gagnon, Montréal district, 1937-1964)

My own job wasn't a very nice one when I started—it was dumping bags. I would take a bag from the corner, open it and dump it on the table, where there were three clerks. I tell you it was hard work, lifting bags. (Paul-Émile Bourassa, Québec district, 1946-1971)

Port aux Basques-to-St. John's run, 1966

Courtesy of Edgar Skanes, St. John's, Newfoundland (St. John's district, 1946-1968)

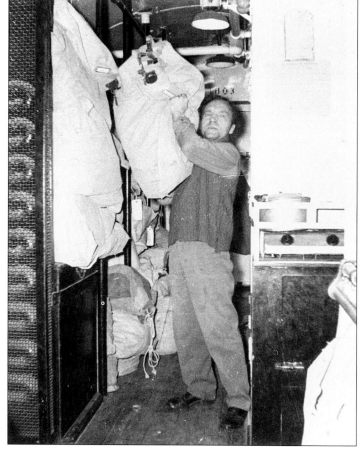

On this one particular run— Toronto, London to Windsor— they had one case on the side; the case was at the end of the coach, you see, and on this one side here they had the letter-carrier walks for Windsor. And this one clerk would sort from Toronto right on through, would sort the mail for the letter-carrier walks in Windsor and then when it would arrive at 7:15 in the morning, then they bundled them up and they would be sent down to the different walks so they would get the mail that same morning for delivery. You see, it was very, very good, efficient service that way.

(Harold Victor Holland, London district, 1946-1949)

With trains, mail could be switched from one route to another at railway transfer points in the open countryside—a great advantage. Mail could thus travel in a more direct line to its destination, avoiding the bottlenecks of city terminals.

Clerks on the main railway lines had to know the distribution points not only for their own postal district, but for bordering districts as well. Much of their work consisted of "forward sortation"—preparing the mail for delivery in other divisions. This greater knowledge earned main-line clerks a higher pay than their branch-line colleagues. Some clerks on the main lines sorted mail only for the city at the other end of the line, breaking the mail down into letter-carrier routes. This yielded a very efficient delivery system where mail could easily be received between major centres the day after posting.

When travelling from Montréal to Toronto, we sorted; coming from Toronto, we...had 140-odd case separations in the train, where we sorted the letters. Apart from the postal stations, we sorted mail for about seventy-five letter carriers in downtown Montréal, so that when we arrived next morning in Montréal the carriers had their mail right away and could take it straight downtown for delivery.

(Irénée Gagnon, Montréal district, 1937-1964)

When you first started out, junior meant dump, that meant the dirty job. You worked at the door, slugged all the mail in, piled it in the stanchions and dispatched it, and you also dumped the bags at the table for the people, turning it upside down to make sure you have all the registrations.

(Bruce F. Greenaway, London district, 1949-1965)

Loading the mail car at Union Station, Toronto, circa 1920

Courtesy of the National Archives of Canada (C 53681)

A mail clerk in the Ottawa district, circa 1945, sorts "blind." He knows the layout of his sorting case so well that he does not need to label the pigeon holes with their destinations. On branch lines the "header" labels on the pigeon holes corresponded to towns along the route where the mail was dropped off, while on main lines the mail was more likely to be sorted according to cities, provinces, or other railway post offices.

Courtesy of the National Archives of Canada (PA 122579)

When we took a parcel and it said Lamartine-sur-mer, we were so used to knowing where the compartment for Lamartine-sur-mer was that we just threw it over and it dropped in. Apart from that, over time we acquired a degree of dexterity; if we'd been in the circus we would have won prizes, we were so good at tossing parcels long distances, because I remember there were some trains with really long racks, but we rarely missed. We set up for the shot like in basketball—off she went into the basket.

(Roger Picard, Québec district, 1948-1952)

Newspapers and parcels are sorted directly into non-locking "tie sacks," Ottawa district, 1938. The wooden "cages" above the row of mailbags served as extensions of the bag racks. Mail clerks "threw upstairs" into these compartments.

Courtesy of the National Archives of Canada (C53693)

This full-length mail car crewed by six men, circa 1925, is likely travelling a main line. Notice the twine dangling from spools mounted on top of the sorting case, the striped mailbag for registered mail, and the leather travel bag on the top storage shelf. Chains hang from the belt loops of men in the foreground to secure the keys for opening bag locks.

Courtesy of the National Archives of Canada (PA 168227)

Registered mailbags were not only locked, but sealed. Twine was wrapped around the bag's middle and, in the early years, secured with red sealing wax. During the twentieth century, the ends of twine were threaded through a piece of lead imprinted with the name of the railway post office and clamped shut using a special press.

National Postal Museum 1990.33.12, 1974.2079.6

Photograph by Claire Dufour

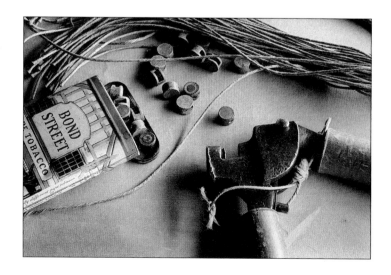

Copy for Book

REFERENCE NO. 16555
Circular No. 1210

7.19 **Post Office Department, Canada**

GENERAL SUPERINTENDENT OF POSTAL SERVICE

OFFICE OF
THE CHIEF SUPERINTENDENT
RAILWAY MAIL SERVICE

Ottawa, January 19, 1933.

All District Superintendents
of Postal Service.

A recent report received in the Department in
connection with the loss of mail keys would lead the
Department to believe that Railway Mail Clerks are
not obeying the regulation which provides that Railway
Mail Service employees on duty must always have the
mail keys attached to their clothing by a safety chain.
When off duty, they must be secured in such a manner
as to be inaccessible to unauthorized persons.

This matter should be again brought to the attention of all Railway Mail Clerks in the District and it
should be pointed out particularly, that the fine for
the loss of mail keys is as follows:-

For the first offence, fine of three days pay.
For the second offence, fine of one week's pay.
For the third offence:- Question of retention
in the service will receive consideration.

The Department feels justified in enforcing this
regulation in all cases, in view of the serious results
which may follow the loss of mail keys should they fall
into the hands of a dishonest person. Railway Mail
Clerks can avoid the loss of keys and the consequent
disciplinary action by complying with this regulation
at all times.

Copy to Secretary
   "   "   Inspection Service,
   "   "   Financial Superintendent,
   "   "   Mr. Coolican,
   "   "   Post Office Service.

Chief Superintendent,
Railway Mail Service.

*Mail clerks are reminded to be more vigilant with their keys in this departmental
circular, 1933.*[51]

Courtesy of the National Archives of Canada

The markings on canvas mailbags served to identify the kind of mail stored inside. Narrow red and white stripes on a locking bag, for example, signified registered mail, while wide stripes on a tie sack denoted parcel post. Notice the "graffiti" mailbag in the foreground.

National Postal Museum 1974.2321.1, 1976.67.1, 1976.71.1, 1976.99.1, 1976.209.1, 1984.96.1

Photograph by Claire Dufour

Close-up of the back of the graffiti mailbag. This bag is a remarkable example of how postal crews communicated with one another during the 1930s. In the decade that this bag remained in circulation, it acquired the autographs, greetings, and artistic renderings of mail handlers across Canada.

National Postal Museum 1976.209.1

Photograph by Claire Dufour

Postmarking instruments: cancelling hammers from various railway post offices; "Registered mail" marker; felt ink pad in wooden case; steel date type in metal case; and a rubber stamping cushion. The facing slips were used by mail clerk W.G. Jones on the Moose Jaw and Shaunavon railway post office, 1951.

National Postal Museum
1974.2079.2, 1974.2079.3,
1974.1071.15, 1990.30.12,
1990.30.16, 1990.34.26

Photograph by Claire Dufour

CANCELLING THE MAIL

Most of the mail that arrived on board had already been date-stamped. Before leaving the post office for the station, each piece of mail would have received a marking, which cancelled the stamp so it could not be reused and identified the date and place of mailing.

> Generally, whatever we received had been cancelled by the post office...But we also had a hammer, that's what we called it, a hammer, which was marked with the name of the train and 'Railway Post Office'....We had a box, a metal box like this with all our equipment inside, and stamps that had to be changed. If there was mail in the box that had been posted in the evening or overnight, it was stamped by that hammer. We also used the hammer when we received registered letters. Suppose we'd got a registered letter from the Gracefield post office for Ottawa, well, we would always stamp the back of it, so if it got lost before it was delivered in Ottawa, they could follow its route according to the transfer bill...

(Paul Sarault, Montréal district, 1952-1958)

Some railway mail clerks had their own rubber handstamps. When they stamped the facing slips they put with each bundle of sorted letters, their work was identified. This "transport marker" kit belonged to Albert Duchesneau, who worked in the Québec district from 1928 to 1958.

Gift of Albert Duchesneau

National Postal Museum 1987.41

Photograph by Steve Darby

Railway mail clerks had to use their cancelling hammers on only two occasions: to date-stamp registered mail and letters dropped through the mail slot in the side of the postal car or collected from the mailbox at train stations. During the early years of the railway mail service, in the mid-1800s, clerks date-stamped every piece of mail they sorted, not just the registers.

> We used to have a letter slot open in the mail car, open to the public. It is just like a little slot that lifts up and drops the letter in....Some came to Truro, rushing: "I didn't get this in the mail—you see that it gets to Halifax tonight!" That was common, we took these letters, opened the mailbag and put them wherever they belonged.
>
> *(Frank C. Peebles, Halifax district, 1945-1971)*

Letters are registered to allow their passage through the system to be tracked. Each clerk applies a postmark to the registered mail and, in this way, if the letter disappears from the mail stream, its point of disappearance can be determined. As soon as a bag of registered mail arrived on board a railway mail car, the clerk would promptly empty its contents along with the "registered letter bill" and would match the contents of the bag with the names on the list. Next, he would date-stamp the back of each envelope, taking care to "tie" the flap to the envelope with his mark as a way of documenting that the seal had not been broken.

CIRCULAR NO. 1157   Post Office Department, Canada.
                                         Postal Service Branch,
File No. 23559   Railway Mail Service.

5.20   O t t a w a, May 27th, 1927.

All District Supts.

                    Date-Stamping Bag Labels and Facing Slips.
                    ───

            Personal observation by the undersigned during recent
trips in various R.P.O's indicates that Railway Mail Clerks are
not carrying out the instructions given in Book of Instructions,
1920, Clause 76, Par: (a) to (h) inclusive.

            Par. (h) is intended to cover an emergency only. It is
evident that some clerks are making the practice of writing
facing slips and bag labels too general and are not even careful
in writing or printing the slips and labels so prepared. The
District Superintendent, his office staff and all Railway Mail
Clerks will readily appreciate the statement that failure to use
printed facing slips and labels, carefully date-stamped and
plainly initialled, slows up handling and sortation, leads to
errors and in the latter event makes tracing difficult, if not
impossible.

            The remedy lies in co-operation and adequate supplies
prepared in advance. (77f).

            Effective, as soon as may be arranged, the District
Superintendent will issue instructions that every Railway Mail
Clerk in his district, running in charge of an R.P.O. or who has
occasion to use labels or slips, who has not already done so, will
provide himself with a rubber dating stamp bearing:-

    (1) The name of the R.P.O. in which he is operating.

    (2) His name in distinct type.

    (3) Movable type to indicate train numbers and date.

            The District Superintendent will submit a statement to
this Service advising if and when these instructions are carried
out.
            He will also instruct the Inspector of Postal Service
(RMS) or any other official making Inspection and reporting on
Form 57 R.M.S. to direct particular attention to Question 18.
            This procedure is to be followed up with careful
checking of results.

                              Chief Superintendent of
                                Railway Mail Service.

A circular admonishes railway mail clerks on the correct use of date stamps and orders them to acquire personal handstamps, 1927.

Courtesy of the National Archives of Canada[52]

Clerks used this same instrument to stamp the facing slip that accompanied each bundle of sorted letters. The name of the railway post office provided a means of tracing back to the guilty crew any mail that had been missorted. As postal officials were quick to reprimand clerks who repeatedly made sorting mistakes, the clerk was kept on his toes.

In the equipment box provided to each mail crew, clerks stored their cancelling hammers, ink pad and ink, and the steel type used to change the date daily. During the nineteenth century, clerks were required to change the time on the hour as well. (More will be said on the appearance of railway postmarks in the chapter on *Postal Markings*.)

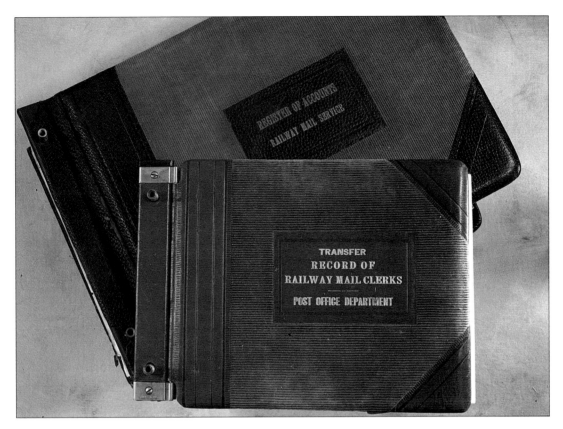

FORMS

Clerks processed a steady flow of paperwork, in addition to the continual stream of mail they handled. Forms were the single means of documenting the often complex routes followed by mail. The clerk-in-charge was assigned the primary responsibility for completing the account of registered mail, requesting overflow storage space for mailbags in the baggage car, preparing the trip report, and reporting on irregularities.

> The clerk-in-charge would come down with his registered mail just before the train was to pull out and he would set up his case and look after the registered mail and any paperwork that was necessary, such as arranging for space in the baggage car and the report on the trip and keeping track of the registered mail and so on.
>
> (Robert Strachan, Winnipeg district, 1946-1966)

Two handsome registers, the Transfer Record of Railway Mail Clerks, 1910, and the Register of Accounts, 1935, document the movement of clerks and money in the railway mail service during the early twentieth century.

National Postal Museum 1974.1578 and 1974.1673.1

Photograph by Claire Dufour

While the rest of the crew sorts mail, the clerk-in-charge completes the forms that will communicate essential information to other crews and postal administrators regarding the mail handled inside this car, circa 1925.

Courtesy of the National Archives of Canada (PA 129700)

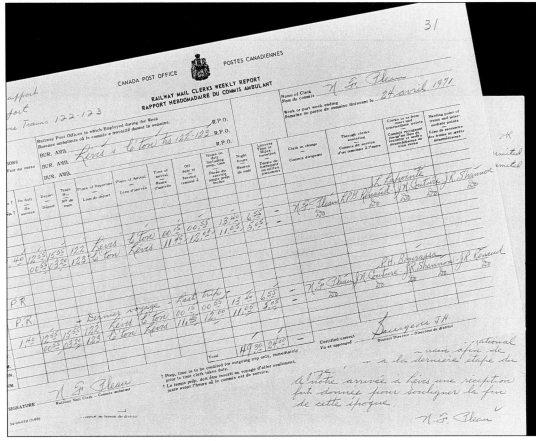

This Railway Mail Clerk's Weekly Report, Campbellton-Lévis run, dated April 24, 1971, provides information on this railway post office's historic last week of operations.

National Postal Museum 1990.27.1-2. Photograph by Steve Darby

RAILWAY MAIL CLERK'S WEEKLY REPORT.

Journal of Duty performed by _R. D. Keron_ employed as Railway Mail Clerk on the _Cal & Van_
Railway for the week ended _sixth_ day of _October_ 1917.

DATE	LEFT PLACE	A.M. Rwy. Time	A.M. Actual Time	P.M. Rwy. Time	P.M. Actual Time	ARRIVED PLACE	A.M. Rwy. Time	A.M. Actual Time	P.M. Rwy. Time	P.M. Actual Time	No. of Miles Travelled DAY	No. of Miles Travelled NIGHT	CLERK IN CHARGE	CLERK ASSISTING
SUNDAY	Calgary			18.25	19.00								Walker	Hitchcock to Vancouver / Hodges Winslow & Self to Golden
MONDAY	Golden	5.24	5.24			Golden / Calgary	12.7	3.43	14.20	14.20	154	190	Ausley	Casselman from Van. / Hodges, Winslow / & Self from Golden
TUESDAY														
WEDNESDAY	Calgary			18.25	18.25								Booth	Martin to Vanc. / Self to Golden
THURSDAY	Golden	5.24	5.24			Golden / Calgary	12.7	12.7	14.20	14.20	169	175	McNames	Mills from Van. / Self from Golden
FRIDAY														
SATURDAY	Calgary	5.55	5.55			Golden			12.47	12.47	156	188	Brown	Smith to Vancouver / Self to Golden
SUNDAY	Golden			16.45	16.45	Calgary	1.25	1.25			479	353	Walker	Burntall from Van. / Self from Golden / Winslow from Banff

N.B.—Full explanations to be given in event of any absence from duty during the week. Any casualty or irregularity to be noted on the back.
The mileage to be divided at the nearest station to or from which the train is running, whether at 8 a.m. or 8 p.m., and not to be computed from any point between two stations.

SUPERINTENDENT'S OBSERVATIONS:

Certified, _____ Supt. Railway Mail Service.

Signature _____ Railway Mail Clerk.

☞ This Report to be sent by first post following close of week to the Superintendent under whose supervision he serves, to be by him transmitted to the Postmaster General for Controller Railway Mail Service, having first been stamped with the date of receipt and certified to by the Superintendent.

19 R. M. S. 100,000-14-8-16.

RAILWAY POST OFFICE
LETTER BILL.

Stamp of _____

From _____
For _Ashcroft Station_
Date _____ 18 _____

Stamp of _____ ASHCROFT STATION B.C.

Despatching Clerk. _____

Receiving Office. _____

Unpaid _____ Cents.

No. _2_ Registered Articles.

McLeod
Clerk in Charge.

Registered No.	NAME.	PLACE.	Where sent by Receiving Clerk.
1.			✓
2.			✓
3.			
4.			
5.			
6.			
7.			

The Railway Mail Clerk's Weekly Report documents business transacted on the Calgary-to-Vancouver run for the week ending October 6, 1917.

National Postal Museum
1974.2088.1

Photograph by Steve Darby

Railway Post Office Letter Bill, prepared by Mr. McLeod, clerk-in-charge for the dispatch of mail at Ashcroft Station, along the Canadian Pacific Railway in British Columbia, June 4-5, 1890

National Postal Museum
1974.2087

Photograph by Steve Darby (Detail)

Metal strongboxes held mail-handling supplies. When not in use, the box was supposed to be stored at the local post office. The initials on this lid stand for "Railway Mail Car."

National Postal Museum 1988.60.1

Photograph by Claire Dufour

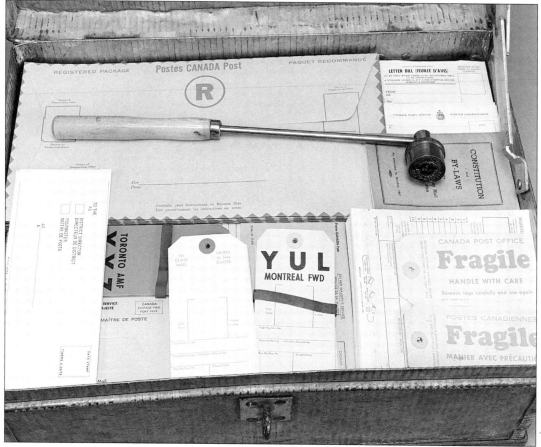

When this metal supply box was unlocked at the National Postal Museum in 1989, it was found to contain all the forms and supplies required to run the Campbellton-Lévis railway post office! This treasure had not been touched since April 24, 1971.

National Postal Museum 1974.2079.1-48.   Photograph by Steve Darby

A mailbag reinforced with leather and a tempered-glass face mask are two distinctive artifacts of the catchpost service.

National Postal Museum
1976.132 and 1989.3.22

Photograph by Claire Dufour

CATCHPOST

Of all the operations of the railway mail service, only one practice was unique to this transportation service alone, the system of collecting mailbags while on a moving train, using the catchpost/catch-arm system.

At one time catchposts were a familiar sight beside rural railway tracks. Situated at points where the track passed near a town and at stations where the train had no scheduled stop, the catchpost was a way of taking on mail as the train sped by. A postmaster or courier delivered the town's mail to the catchpost, secured the mailbag, and waited for the train.

This photograph shows a successful catch at Goward, Ontario, circa 1960.

Courtesy of Don Smith, North Bay, Ontario

As the mail car roared by, the railway mail clerk manoeuvred a catch arm mounted on the side of the car to catch the incoming mailbag. At the same time he threw the outgoing mailbag onto the ground. He had to be careful to aim his throw so as not to injure anyone, and to throw the bag far enough that it would not be pulled under the train as it sped by. All this required good timing and skill on the part of the railway mail clerk, who was known to miss the catch occasionally.

A special mailbag was designed for the catchpost service. This bag was reinforced with leather strapping to support the weight of the mail inside when the bag was suspended from a catchpost. When the railway mail service had come to an almost complete halt in 1967, inmates at the Kingston Penitentiary were assigned the task of converting these catchpost bags to first-class mail use by removing the leather strapping.[53]

> The catchpost was at places where the train didn't stop. It was a special bag of tougher, reinforced canvas with leather straps that were a little longer; the mail was put in that, and it was hung straight up on a pole. We had a metal arm about so big. When we were getting there, we had landmarks, places where we could determine that we were getting close. At that point we would pull on the handle and raise the catch arm; and as we came by...the bag would be lowered down and brought in.
>
> *(Paul Sarault, Montréal district, 1952-1958)*

Postal authorities recognized early on that there were inherent problems with this system that were above and beyond the control of the railway mail clerks. If the train didn't slow down, if steam, smoke or cinders were blowing into the clerk's face, if visibility was poor due to bad weather, or if the catch-arm mechanism was not working perfectly, a catch could easily be missed or dropped.

"Catching" the mail could be a hazardous occupation. Many a clerk's eye was left smarting or even permanently scarred from hot cinders blown from the locomotive's funnel towards the clerk poised at the open door to make a catchpost connection. A tempered-glass face mask was stored inside the mail car, ready to be hooked onto the door frame to provide a shield between the burning embers and the clerk's face. Alternatively, the clerk could wear plastic goggles.

Some unfortunate railway mail clerks lost a finger to the catch arm, thereby gaining admission to the "missing finger" club of catchpost operators. Trains were required to slow down to twenty miles per hour (thirty-two km) for the catch, but former railway mail clerks report that engineers often disregarded this regulation.

Engineers were also requested to signal approaching catchposts by pulling on the whistle, but it was up to the mail clerk to develop his own system of landmarks to alert him to impending catchposts. Such landmarks could be as basic as a hay wagon parked

Ottawa 6 Oct 1870

Sir,

I have the honor to report that I left the Prescott Station on 12 Sept 1870 at 12:05 p.m. for the west, Mr. Menzies was the Railway Mail Clerk in charge. I found on the train the new bag catcher... The English apparatus [used in England] catches the bag in a net, whilst that in use here (copied I believe from the one employed in the United States) grasps the bag in an iron fork which catches the bag by the impetus of the train. It will be found a task of much difficulty by the Railway Mail Clerks to ascertain the time of passing the station at which the bag is to be caught, or on dark and stormy nights, and during piercingly cold weather when the car will be chilled by having the door open...It is true that gong bells are attached to the ceiling of the Postal Car for the purpose of giving notice when nearing a station, to which a line is run from the Engineer...

Excerpt from a report by Post Office Inspector Bucke to the Postmaster General on the catchpost service introduced in 1870.[54]

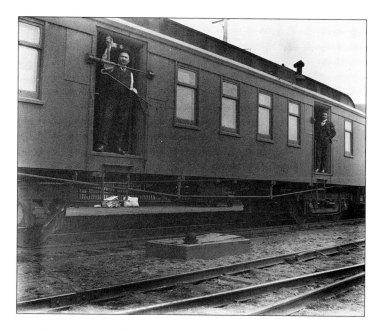

The catch arm folds against the doorway when not in use, circa 1920.

Courtesy of the National Archives of Canada (PA 98498)

in a farmer's field. If the farmer decided to move the wagon, the clerk might miss his catch!

Many a droll tale is told by former railway mail clerks of catches that were missed: how mailbags landed in snowbanks and couldn't be found till spring, or how they landed in boxcars parked on a railway siding. At the time of the incident, of course, the story was not so funny. Because the Post Office was held at fault for failing to deliver, the blame landed squarely on the shoulders of the clerk. Forms had to be filled out, investigations conducted, and searches undertaken.

> Somewhere up in northern Ontario on the CP, the train was supposed to make a catch at a certain point, but the train never slowed down. And there was a lot of money shipped in those days, so the catch bag had a double bottom because of the fact that they [*sic*] had to take the strength of the catch. And of course everything would go to the bottom of the bags. But anyway the train never slowed down and the clerk tried to make the catch at about seventy miles an hour [113 km], and anyway the money bag just went straight out the bottom of the bag, and he said he could hear the coins clinking down the track.
>
> (*Michael Millar, Toronto district, 1965-1971*)

Copy for the Book.

CIRCULAR NO. 1090   POST OFFICE DEPARTMENT, CANADA.

FILE NO. 20988   POSTAL SERVICE BRANCH,
                                  Railway Mail Service.

3.20   OTTAWA, December 29th, 1925.

All District Supts.

            Complaint has again been received at the Department that a passenger on a station platform has been injured through the careless despatch of mails from a moving train. The District Superintendent will, therefore, renew the instructions to all Railway Mail Clerks in his District that every precaution must be taken when despatching mail bags to avoid injury to people who may be on the station platform. Mails must not be thrown from moving trains to the station platform at points where the train is scheduled to stop until the train ceases motion.

            When despatching mails at catching post points the clerks should exercise great care and judgment, and when the ground conditions are favourable mails should be despatched while approaching the post and not thrown on the platform for the convenience of the mail courier.

            Further, a great many Clerks when despatching and receiving mails at Catch Offices stand altogether too far back from the door. As a result they cannot see properly where to deliver the mails, nor is the bag on the post in constant vision, therefore it is not possible to give the catching arm the proper elevation, consequently bags are frequently missed which should be picked up.

                        Chief Superintendent of
                          Railway Mail Service.

Clerks are reminded of the proper procedure to be followed at catchpost points, 1925.

Courtesy of the National Archives of Canada[55]

In 1933, 114 catchposts were in use in Canada; by 1967, there were only ten. Today, the only evidence that remains to indicate that this remarkable technology ever existed is the occasional presence of a solitary weathered post beside the railway track, deep in the countryside.

A courier positions the mailbag on the catchpost minutes before the train arrives, circa 1950.

Courtesy of the Canadian Postal Archives (POS 2380)

As the train rolls by the catchpost, an anonymous arm reaches out to snare the bag in this close-up view.

Courtesy of the Canadian Postal Archives (POS 2400)

The last mail delivery by train at Coldbrook, Nova Scotia, 1956.

Notice the mail clerk kicking the outgoing bag onto the ground as he snares the incoming bag from the catchpost.

Courtesy of the Canadian Postal Archives (POS 2396) (Detail)

Bags despatched at 'catch' stations must not be kicked off but must be thrown off by hand and to a sufficient distance from the track so as to prevent their being drawn under the train.

(Instructions to Railway Mail Clerks, 1910)[56]

Receiving the Message

The Post Office's task is not complete until the correspondence has been safely received at its destination. Householder mail receptacles come in an assortment of shapes and sizes, relating to different delivery methods and to style changes over time. The following photographs present historical views of mail reception and some examples of nineteenth-century mail receivers from the collection of the National Postal Museum.

These signs portray the changing graphic identity of the Canadian Post Office over the years.

National Postal Museum 1974.2249.1, 1974.2245.1, 1974.2244.1, 1974.2250.1, 1974.2201.1, 1984,160.1, 1985.249.17, 1974.2243.1, 1974.2242.1, 1974.2207.1, 1974.2200.1

Photograph by Claire Dufour

Just off train 61, the mail waits on the station platform at Balcarres, Saskatchewan, to be delivered to the local post office and into the waiting hands of readers, 1959.

Courtesy of the Canadian Postal Archives (POS 2398)

Subscribers receive their Ottawa newspaper without delay at the Vernon, Ontario, post office, which is housed inside the general store, 1947.

Courtesy of the National Archives of Canada (C 53549)

John Phillips receives the mail at the Vernon, Ontario, post office for delivery to rural addresses, 1947.

Courtesy of the National Archives of Canada (PA 61686, C 53545)

The letter carrier slips the mail through the slot in the front door of this distinguished-looking address, circa 1925.

Courtesy of the National Archives of Canada (PA 129682)

Impatient to read his mail, this gentleman lingers at the lock box he rents at the post office in his urban community, circa 1920. Customers without letter-carrier or rural delivery have always collected their mail directly from the post office. Lock boxes are made available at larger post offices for clients who prefer a private mailbox to "general delivery," which is handed through the wicket by the postmaster.

Courtesy of the National Archives of Canada (PA 61977)

Do you know this address? Somewhere, rural Canada.

Courtesy of the Canadian Postal Archives (POS 2392)

This elegant bank of lock boxes would have graced an urban Canadian post office over one hundred years ago. Made by the Yale Lock Company, the brass filigree doors bear the initials of Queen Victoria (Victoria Regina).

National Postal Museum 1974.2133.1

Photograph by Claire Dufour

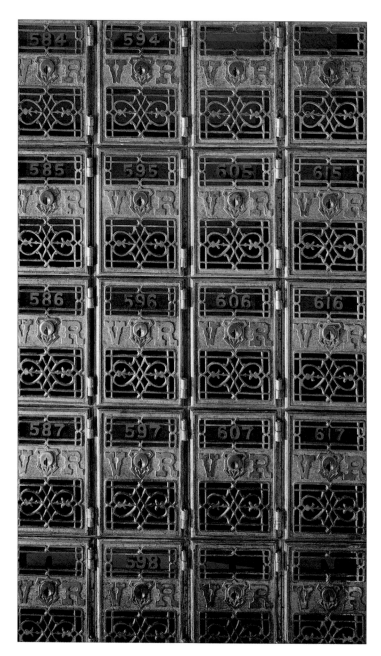

About as old as Canadian Confederation, each of the 101 cast-brass doors in this bank of post office lock boxes displays a stylized beaver. The "money order" inscription written in French inside the wicket opening suggests a Quebec provenance.

National Postal Museum
1991.37.1

Photographs by Claire Dufour

Letter-carrier service came to the city of Québec in 1875, at which time the Post Office urged its customers to provide mail receptacles such as this outside their homes.

National Postal Museum
1985.189.1

Photograph by Claire Dufour

CANADA

POST OFFICE DEPARTMENT

Post Office Department
Canada

OFFICE OF
THE CHIEF SUPERINTENDENT
RAILWAY MAIL SERVICE

To whom it may Concern:

THE BEARER

E. Melnyk

is a Railway Mail Clerk authorized to travel
in Postal Cars on duty

In Edmonton District

Chief Superintendent,
Railway Mail Service

Ottawa, Canada, Jan'y 3rd 1939

Approved

Deputy Postmaster General

No. O-22

Signature of Railway Mail Cl'k

Officially identified,

R. W. Hale.

District Superintendent
of Postal Service

Railway
in Postal

Edmonton District

Chief Superintendent,
Railway Mail Service

awa, Canada, 2nd March 1946

ved

N.E. Atwater

Deputy Postmaster General

Officially identified.

Thos. J. Reilly

District Superintendent
of Postal Service

The Railway Mail Clerk

SECTION 3
ON TRACK

Who Were the Railway Mail Clerks?

Railway mail clerks considered themselves a unique breed of employee. While they were being interviewed as part of the research for the **On Track** exhibition, they were asked to describe themselves. According to them, the typical clerk was an independent worker, yet a team player; an individualist who loved freedom, sought adventure, and possessed a sense of wanderlust; was sociable; physically fit; competitive; ambitious; and had an excellent memory. Certainly, these words seem to suit the men who spent their working lives roving the country in mobile post offices, stamping, sorting and catching the mail.

An employee handbook printed in 1952, *You and Your Post Office*, describes these men and their work:

> It will be apparent that these men form a very important link in the postal chain of communications, being required to sort and make up the mail against time, and—by their knowledge of plane and train connections—to give it the most expeditious routing....While the working conditions... are not to be compared with those in the average post office, there is the compensation of higher pay, self reliance and adventure of travel.[57]

The men not only had to be fit, but under the age of thirty-five (prior to 1920 the age was thirty years) when they started out, a regulation probably intended to initiate

OPPOSITE PAGE:

Strangers with a face. This collection of pass cards identifies some of the men who worked as railway mail clerks. Issued as a security measure, the passes were voided when the men left the Service.

National Postal Museum 1981.20.1, 1987.47.1, 1987.49.1, 1989.27.1, 1990.31.2-9

Photograph by Claire Dufour

You felt that you were part of a team, a very small team, and while you didn't feel superior to anybody else, you felt that you had a really important part to play in the mail service. (Harold Victor Holland, London district, 1946-1949)

Original photographic composition by J.-E. Livernois, 1924

National Postal Museum 1991.36.1

Gift of Réal Cameron, Sainte-Foy, Quebec

Photograph by Steve Darby

the men into the physically demanding work while their backs were still strong. From 1882 until about 1955, they were required to pass a general aptitude examination administered by the civil service, in order to be considered for employment in the railway mail service or, for that matter, anywhere in the Post Office.[58]

The job security and retirement pension offered by the civil service drew the men to the Post Office, and following the two world wars, veterans were given priority status for employment with government departments such as the Post Office. Clerks often applied to the railway mail service from other mail handling positions in the Post Office, as the railway

We were free! We didn't have any supervisors watching us all the time, we were free! We just had to do our work the way we were supposed to, and nobody bothered us. (Albert Duchesneau, Québec district, 1928-1958)

Courtesy of the Canadian Postal Archives (POS 2394)

mail service constituted a promotion, and during the twentieth century, it offered a higher rate of pay than the "inside" positions. Often the men started out as relief clerks, replacing those who were sick or on vacation, before being hired full time. The Service had a romantic appeal that attracted men of a non-conformist nature.

Women were never hired to work as mail clerks on the trains.[59] This was likely because the close quarters on board permitted no room for privacy; the lugging of thirty-four kilogram-plus (seventy-five lb.) mailbags demanded a robust physique that women were thought not to possess; and, generally, because the Post Office was not in the habit of hiring women for heavy mail handling during the years that the railway mail service was active.

Former clerks speak about the strong sense of *esprit de corps* they shared. Because the men often worked together for years on the same crew, squeezed into the cramped quarters of the mail car and camping out in these same quarters, or booking into a hotel on the nights they were on duty and the trains made long stopovers, a close bond inevitably developed among them. Their day-to-day business contact was limited to themselves and members of the train crew, involving little contact with other postal employees. Many railway mail clerks proudly thought

We kind of believed in ourselves. We believed that we were the best and because we believed, we were! (Bruce Greenaway, London district, 1949-1965)

First run of the Prince George to Prince Rupert railway post office, September, 1914

Courtesy of the Canadian Postal Archives (POS 2386)

of themselves as a cut above the average postal worker. Along with knowing more distribution points in the postal network than their "inside" counterparts, they were able to perform their tasks under less-than-ideal physical conditions.

> For myself, I enjoyed the twenty-seven-and-a-half years I spent on the 'road.' The job was challenging, adventurous and never dull. I have travelled well over a million miles over much of Manitoba and parts of Saskatchewan, Minnesota and northwestern Ontario, through beautiful country and in all imaginable kinds of weather, and I have met many people I would never otherwise have learned to know and appreciate. It is now sixteen years

We took pride in handling the people's mail. (Stanley A. Martin, Winnipeg district, 1947-1966)

Courtesy of the Canadian Postal Archives (POS 2367)

since the demise of the R.M.S. [Railway Mail Service], the most efficient system of mail distribution ever devised. But, to attest to the camaraderie it engendered amongst its members, those of us who survive still meet once a month for luncheon and to recall the good old days of a bygone era. I can only say I am proud to have been a member of that vanished breed.

(A.J. Janssens, Winnipeg district, 1943-1971)[60]

Twenty and thirty years later, former clerks still fraternize together on a regular basis.

Printed in 1909, this personnel assessment form casts a probing and paternalistic eye on the work of the railway mail clerk.

Courtesy of the National Archives of Canada[61]

Clerks, in their official intercourse with the public and with one another, must observe the strictest courtesy, and must endeavor, by active and intelligent efforts, to promote the efficiency of the service. Discussions and loud talk when at work must be avoided.

Extract from Instructions to Railway Mail Clerks *(section 25), 1906*

R.M.S.

_____ District

_____ 19 ....

STATEMENT concerning _____

_____ a Railway Mail Clerk now stationed

at _____

_____

1. Married or single? _____

2. If married, number of children? _____

3. Age of children under 21 years? _____

4. Is his eyesight good? _____

5. Has he a good memory? _____

6. Is he industrious or indolent? _____

7. Does he show aptitude for the Service? _____

8. Does he take any interest in the Service? _____

9. Is he ready and willing to obey regulations, instructions and orders? _____

10. Is he careful and neat, or careless and slovenly in doing his work? _____

11. Is he slow or quick? _____

12. Does he learn his distribution slowly or readily? _____

13. What is his physical condition? _____

14. Does he read the address on mail matter readily? _____

15. Is he noisy or talkative on duty? _____

16. Is he addicted to the use of intoxicating liquors? _____

17. Is he apparently doing his utmost to succeed? _____

18. Does he keep his car clean and orderly? _____

19. Is it your opinion that he is a suitable person for the service, and one who would be promoted to a more responsible position? _____

20. Do you (if probationary) recommend his permanent appointment? _____

REMARKS.

_____

_____

_____

_____

_____

_____

_____

_____

Supt. R.M.S.

71 R.M.S. - 3000-1 1909

Training and Advancement

The careers of railway mail clerks usually began on branch lines, where they manipulated the heavy, dirty mailbags for the other clerks, or worked as relief clerks, replacing clerks on leave. As a relief clerk, the neophyte could get to know a postal district well, travelling whenever (especially holidays) and wherever his assistance was required. This was where he got his training, learning by example the varied tasks of the job.

When he was hired, the clerk was issued a set of manuals, keys and a temporary pass. Clerks were given six months to memorize the contents of the *Distribution Book* and the *Schedule of Mail Trains* for their districts and to learn the rules and regulations spelled out in the *Official Postal Guide* and *Instructions to Railway Mail Clerks*. Then, they were tested.

The most stressful component of the job was the case examination. Using a special sorting case, clerks

Passing the annual sortation examination was so important, clerks such as J.D. McDermott bought their own exam case to practise at home.

National Postal Museum 1987.46.1

Gift of J.D. McDermott, Saint John, New Brunswick (Saint John district, 1945-1969)

Photographs by Claire Dufour

Justus Webster's record-breaking performance on the Alberta-British Columbia major case examination made The Lethbridge Herald *newspaper in 1948. The* Railway Mail Clerk *magazine reported that the previous record had stood for three decades. Mr. Webster beat his own time a few years later.*

Courtesy of The Lethbridge Herald *and Mary Webster, Lethbridge, Alberta*

SATURDAY, JULY 31, 1948

SETS NEW RECORD
✦ ✦ ✦　　　✦ ✦ ✦　　　✦ ✦ ✦
HONORS GO TO J. F. WEBSTER

J. F. Webster of the city, is cause for the Lethbridge post office department sticking a feather in its cap.

Mr. Webster set an unsurpassed record in speed and accuracy for the Dominion in case examinations held in February in sorting mail. He received 100% on the test, sorting 1,000 cards in the record time of 16 minutes and 30 seconds. The last record set was by a London, Ont., man who did the exam in 17 minutes and 28 seconds.

A member of the Lethbridge post office staff since 1930, Mr. Webster is now a railway postal clerk, which position he assumed in 1942.

All Take Tests

All postal and railway clerk men take the tests, A. Darlington, city postmaster told the Herald Thursday. For them they must know all the distribution centres in their areas. Clerks in this city are tested on Alberta and British Columbia towns and postal centres.

were tested on their ability to direct mail to the appropriate point in the postal network. The objective of the examination was to test the clerk's ability to sort each of the thousand cards printed with a name of a post office into the slot which corresponded to the card's correct distribution point. Clerks were given one hour to complete the examination. The only way to learn the distribution points of a district was to memorize the contents of the *Distribution Book* for that region. If a clerk failed repeatedly to pass the case examination with a minimum ninety per cent grade, he would lose his salary increase and could be discharged altogether.

Furthermore, to ensure that clerks kept abreast of the schedule and routing changes which constantly took place in the postal network, the Post Office administered the case examination annually. Clerks could never slacken their attention. Upon the creation of the Railway Mail Service Department in 1897, statistics on case examination scores began to be published in the annual report of the Postmaster General and, from that year on, a clerk's score became a factor when he was being considered for

J.S. Hillhouse, Winnipeg district, poses in 1951 after having scored one hundred per cent on his case exams for twenty-four consecutive years. Does he look proud! Note the metal equipment box at his feet.

National Postal Museum

promotion. Postal officials acknowledge the benefits of this examination in the following extract from the *Report of the Postmaster General, 1898*:

> Case examinations have also the effect of stimulating the clerks, and exciting amongst them a spirit of friendly rivalry to obtain the highest credit in the general result for the Dominion.[62]

Senior clerks on the main lines were not only required to score at least ninety-seven per cent on the case examination, they were tested on the distribution points for two to three different districts. These clerks were understandably proud of their knowledge and powers of memory.

As the clock counts away the minutes, solemn clerks in solemn attire perform the annual test that will determine whether they get their salary raise or, worse, hold on to their jobs. The examiner behind the desk has prepared the scale and parcels that will test the clerks' knowledge of mailing rates as part of the examination on the Official Postal Guide. *Circa 1920.*

During the 1960s the number of cards to be sorted during the hour was reduced from 1,000 to 500.

Courtesy of the National Archives of Canada (PA 61982)

Railway mail service employee Harry Hall fantasizes about the advantages and disadvantages of being able to use a gramophone to study for his case examinations. Harry Hall began working in the Moose Jaw, Saskatchewan, district in 1914.

Courtesy of the Canadian Postal Archives

Post Office Department

Payroll No. 402
Paylist No. 72

ANNUAL EFFICIENCY REPORT

Date of Last Report 1st January, 1955

Office and Date

LONDON DISTRICT
1st January, 1956

NAME ELGIE, H.T.

1. Date of appointment: Temporary 3rd March, 1942   Permanent 30th June, 1947

2. Present class title Railway Mail Clerk, Grade 1R   Date 10th March, 1952

3. Present salary $ 3,510.00   Date 1st December, 1953

4. New Salary At maximum $ -   Date -

5. Concise statement of duties Railway Mail Clerk - Relief

6. Ratings:—Exceptionally Good.............................. Above Average..............................

   Average X .... Below Average.............. Unsatisfactory..............

7. Explanation of Rating— Good worker, reliable and trustworthy, carries on without much supervision, good knowledge of work but inclined toward overconfidence, has shown improvement in tact and co-operation.

8. Suspensions since last report (State length and reasons) Nil

9. Times late since last report   No. Nil   Time Lost Nil

10. Absences since last report   No. Nil   Days Lost Nil

11. Has employee passed required Departmental examinations during past year? Yes (yes or no) If so,

    27th January, 1955 - 98.7%

Like all railway mail clerks, Harold Elgie's performance was scrutinized and reported upon each year.
National Postal Museum 1974.2323.2. Gift of Harold T. Elgie, London, Ontario (London district, 1942-1964)
Photograph by Steve Darby (Detail)

A set of enamelled tinware speaks of some comforts available to railway mail clerks once their work was done.

National Postal Museum 1988.55.2,3,4,5

Gift of Jean-Marc Taillon, (Québec district, 1948-1961)

Photograph by Claire Dufour

Life on Board

Once the railway mail clerks arrived on board, the first thing they did was change into work clothes. While no official uniform was issued, the unofficial attire was overalls and heavy work boots, and in the 1960s the Post Office began to provide the clerks with overalls. Documents from the latter nineteenth century, however, suggest that the attire could be quite natty back then. Québec's *The Morning Chronicle,* dated December 21, 1877, reads: "It is stated that after the New Year, the postal clerks on the Intercolonial Railway will be allowed a uniform suit, to consist of blue double-breasted sack coat, with brass buttons, blue vest and pants, and naval cap, with a fatigue suit of white overalls and blue flannel shirt."

> I worked mostly out of Calgary on the day train and that train came in about 7:30 every morning, so that meant that you had to get up early...[W]e always had what we call the bullpen, where we checked in and went to read the orders. Our orders

were always sent from Vancouver to us...Many times in the old days the old steam pots— especially during the winter months in the prairies— the trains were always late. That was one of the things you had to put up with as a railway mail clerk, you should say as a travelling man, in those days.

(Norman Johnston, Calgary district, 1948-1965)

A railway mail clerk's shift did not end when his work was done. On the contrary, he often spent the night in a distant town waiting for the train to begin its return trip home. Once the mail was sorted and bagged and the necessary paperwork completed, clerks could relax until the train pulled into the station.

They were given ample provisions for passing this free time. Every clerk carried on board a kitbag full of personal effects and food to see him through the two-to-three-day journey. When not dozing, they idled away the time playing cards or sometimes illicitly reading the magazines and newspapers travelling through the system. Many smoked and even took the odd drop of liquor, both of which were strictly prohibited. Mail cars were equipped with a water tank and small stove for dining on board. A "grub box" held a frying pan, kettle, condiments, tea, canned goods and the like. Paul Sarault (Ottawa district, 1952-1958) says he still boils water for his tea for a sterilizing twenty minutes, a habit acquired on the trains to render the water potable.

A favourite meal staple seems to have been potatoes. One of the more popular anecdotes of former clerks is their description of how they cooked the spuds on top of gas lamps in the days preceding electricity. Men on the branch lines had the advantage of being able to buy fresh food, such as eggs, from farmers at rural train stations. Sometimes the clerks struck an arrangement with these farmers whereby, in return for running errands in town for the farmer, the clerk received fresh produce and game.

The men equipped themselves with blankets and bedrolls on the runs where they were obliged to pass the night camped out on the train, or they could use the "paillasse" (nicknamed pallyass) bedroll provided

To start with, we had a schedule at home that we would look at; it told us the day and time the trains would be leaving...My wife would prepare some kind of lunch for me...We had a big mailbag that held our personal effects, overalls, change of clothes, a cap—we even had a cap— because it was dusty...

(Roger Picard, Québec district, 1948-1952)

...[T]hey were gas lighted, they roasted potatoes very nicely too. Oh yeah, you put a potato on top of those lights and it was lovely in an hour.

(David C. Blackhall, Toronto district, 1950-1970)

by some railway companies. In 1868, railway mail clerks were provided the relative luxury of a sofa! This, along with a washstand and blinds, comprised standard equipment on board the mail car.[63]

When the train pulled into station too late at night to book into a hotel, or if the layover lasted just a short while, clerks simply converted a lumpy pile of mailbags into a makeshift mattress. Rules of hierarchy applied to sleeping accommodation: the clerk-in-charge slept in relative luxury on the sorting-case ledge, and the first assistant on the facing table, relegating the others to the mailbags. Jean-Marc Taillon (Québec district, 1948-1961) likes to tell the story of how he once slept on a million dollars! The mutilated bills were being shipped back to the Royal Canadian Mint in Ottawa.

A travel allowance of one cent per mile, raised to fifteen cents by 1955, covered the cost of hotel and food, with a little left over. Members of a crew who regularly laid over in a specific place often pooled their dollars to rent a room or apartment close to the train station. Or they had a favourite hotel that offered these frequent guests a cheap rate and a permanent reservation. In Montréal, for example, the Queen's Hotel was the preferred home away from home; it was close to the station, inexpensive and friendly.

Sometimes a railway mail clerk only travelled part of the distance of a run, and hopped out at a stop along the way to catch a ride home on the next return train. On the way back, he rode as "dead-head" crew, helping out a little, but mostly just relaxing.

Reading Mail Matter in Transit Forbidden

Clerks must not remove newspapers or other printed matter from their wrappers, packages, or bundles for the purpose of reading the same.

Extract from Instructions to Railway Mail Clerks (section 34) 1906[64]

To illustrate the schedule of a typical shift, J.B. Mooney (Québec district, 1930-1965) has provided an example from the Québec-Noranda run, where he worked from 1948 to 1965. Mr. Mooney began his shift at 7:00 p.m., when he arrived on board to set up and begin work; the train pulled out at 8:15 p.m. and travelled through the night, arriving in Noranda at 2:00 p.m. the following day; the return voyage began at 10:00 p.m., and ended at Québec at 7:00 a.m. the next day. According to Mr. Mooney, he was scheduled to

BOOK

Circular No. 1160   POST OFFICE DEPARTMENT,
File Nos. 26016, 12073   Railway Mail Service,
5:23   OTTAWA, August 12, 1927.

All District Superintendents,
     Postal Service,

SAFE GUARDING MAILS.

SMOKING IN POSTAL AND BAGGAGE CARS.

          Reference is made to the frequent and repeated ins-
tructions relative to the question of Railway Mail Clerks smoking
while on duty in Postal Cars and Baggage Cars in Circular 3481,
14 July,'21; Circular 887, 22 June,'22, and particularly Circular 1077, 23 April, 1925.

          The instructions contained in the last mentioned are
being disregarded and such violations must cease.

          The District Superintendent will be good enough to
renew instructions to all concerned to the effect that smoking
of cigarettes is not permissable either in Postal Cars or
Baggage Cars containing mails, whether the train is standing
at station or under motion.

          He will further advise all Inspectors attached to
his Staff who at any time observe violations of these regulations that they are to make a full report of their observations to the Department.

                                        [signature]

                              Chief Superintendent,
                                Railway Mail Service.

Evidently, smoking was a difficult habit for mail clerks to break in the 1920s.
Courtesy of the National Archives of Canada[65]

make one such trip each week. For every five trips,
he was given one trip off, providing a break of several days.[66]

During this scheduled time off, it was not uncommon
for the clerk to take a part-time job, working perhaps
as a handyman, store clerk or security guard (the
postal clerk already possessed a security clearance).

This notice leaves no doubt that liquor was not welcome on board back in 1913.

Courtesy of the National Archives of Canada[67]

POST OFFICE DEPARTMENT, CANADA

OTTAWA, 3rd November, 1913.

SPECIAL CIRCULAR TO RAILWAY MAIL CLERKS.

Railway Mail Clerks have already been notified that they should not take liquor. The Postmaster General has been informed in a general way that in many cases this notice has been disregarded, and whilst he has no desire to take any one unawares, he has given instructions that a general warning be issued to all Railway Mail Clerks that the moment it is credibly reported to him that any railway mail clerk uses liquor, he may as well send in his resignation, because he will be dismissed, and no amount of influence will bring about his re-instatement.

Railway Mail Clerks must understand that on account of the heavy responsibility which rests on them and also that so much money is entrusted to their care in registered letters and otherwise, it is absolutely indispensable that liquor should be discarded entirely.

Railway Mail Clerks must also understand that under no circumstances shall any liquor be carried on a Postal Car, and that no person other than those on duty, as mentioned in the printed instructions to Railway Mail Clerks, shall be permitted to have access to a Postal Car, and that any violation of these rules will lead to instant dismissal.

Each Railway Mail Clerk is instructed to acknowledge the receipt of this Circular to the Department and to add an assurance that he thoroughly understood and is prepared to abide by the instructions which it contains.

By order of the Postmaster General.

R.M. COULTER,

Deputy Postmaster General.

No full-time Postal employee shall engage in any remunerative employment or occupation outside his regular duties unless authority for such employment is received...

This extract from Manual of Instructions to Railway Mail Clerks *(section 6), appears only in the 1955 version.[68]*

Frank Peebles (Halifax district, 1945-1971) found his work schedule so complicated that he kept track of it in pocket diaries, two of which are now in the collection of the National Postal Museum.

Former railway mail clerks spoke about how difficult their long absences could be on the family. Edward Cybulski's (Ottawa district, 1942-1971) first children

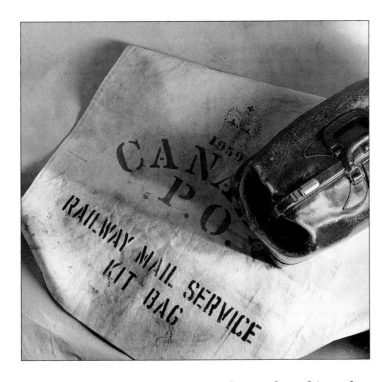

Some clerks provided their own leather travel bags for storing clothing and toiletries. Others simply converted a registered or first-class mailbag to their needs, stencilling it clearly to avoid confusion with bags in service.

National Postal Museum
1988.56.2 (leather bag)

Gift of J. O. A. Duchesneau, Québec, Quebec (Québec district, 1927-1958)

National Postal Museum
1976.156.1

Photograph by Claire Dufour

were born while he was out on the road, and it took Donald McCarthy (Ottawa district, 1958-1971) twenty years to acquire the necessary seniority that would allow him to book off Christmas and New Year's!

Other clerks report that working in a mail car had some long-term positive effects on their lives. Karl Remus (Ottawa district, 1946-1949) reports:

> I was working in Ottawa in 1941 and met a girl from the Upper Ottawa Valley and we dated a few times. But then seven years went by, including my military service, and I didn't see her or hear from her. Then one day I was sorting mail in the postal car of the CPR's transcontinental train between Montréal and North Bay. I happened to run across a letter addressed to this girl and noticed she was still "Miss." A few days later I drove up the valley from Montréal and we renewed acquaintances. A year later, we were married.[69]

'Taking five" on the Campbellton-Lévis run, 1971. Sometimes members of a "deadhead" crew hitched a ride back to their point of origin. As they had no work obligations on this run, they could take it easy.

Courtesy of the Canadian Postal Archives (POS 2402) and Canada Post Corporation

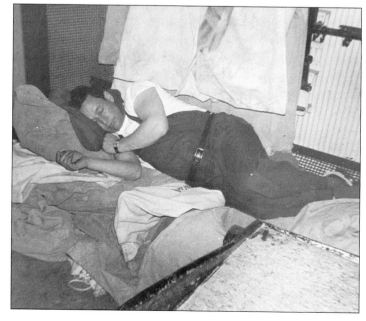

A last lumpy snooze on the last run, Toronto to Ottawa, April 23, 1971

Courtesy of the Canadian Postal Archives (POS 2371) (Detail)

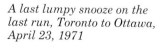

Certainly, the railway mail clerks did not hold nine-to-five desk jobs. But, judging by comments made during the course of oral history interviews, none seemed to mind the odd working hours.

However, during the interviews, former clerks did complain about a litany of factors regarding working conditions: the train shook, jolted and occasionally even derailed; the lighting was poor and sometimes failed altogether, necessitating the use of candles; the quarters were cramped and dusty, with poor ventilation; the cars were too cold in winter, too hot in summer, and always too noisy; and adverse climatic conditions such as blizzards and floods could strand the train and its travellers, including the mail.

Through the Canadian Railway Mail Clerks' Federation (formerly the Dominion Railway Mail Clerks' Federation), clerks lobbied for better working conditions. One of their primary achievements was better lighting, but they had little control over the other factors. This was the unromantic side of life as a railway mail clerk.

The mail car (next to the locomotive) derailed along with the rest of the train in this wreck at Jaffray, British Columbia, 1905.

Courtesy of the Canadian Postal Archives (POS 2368)

Newfoundland railway mail clerks could sleep in style. Their mail cars were equipped with bunks!

Courtesy of Edgar Skanes, St. John's, Newfoundland (St. John's district, 1946-1968)

Railway mail service employee Harry Hall pokes fun at the schoolboy antics that some of his fellow workers could resort to in order to escape extra duty.

Courtesy of the Canadian Postal Archives

Harry Hall produces a chuckle as he looks beyond the romance of the railway mail clerk's vocation to the daily trials.

Courtesy of the Canadian Postal Archives

Arriving home to the welcome sight of an awaiting family, Calgary, 1955

Courtesy of the Canadian Postal Archives (POS 2389) and The Moose Jaw Times-Herald, *Moose Jaw, Saskatchewan*

MAY 10
1858
AUG 9
1854
L.C.
CANADA
CANADA-10-Cts.

Philately

Postal Markings

> Carefully arrange your dated Stamp previous to
> the commencement of your Journey, so that its
> impression will shew [*sic*] the date of your trip and
> the direction in which you are travelling.
>
> All letters received by you en route must be rated
> in plain figures with the postage to which they are
> liable, on the face, at the right hand upper corner
> and must likewise be stamped with your dated
> Stamp on the face at the left-hand lower corner.
>
> All letters passing through your office must be
> postmarked with your dated Stamp on the back.
>
> All Letter Bills received by you must be marked
> with your dated Stamp on the back.
>
> The Time Bill, Account of Mails sent and Received,
> and Registered Letter Sheet must also be marked
> with your dated Stamp.[70]

These instructions were drafted in 1857 to advise
the infant group of railway mail clerks on the proper
procedures for marking the mail. Each railway post
office (R.P.O.) had its name cut into the date stamp.
In the early years, each R.P.O. marking contained
the name of the railroad it travelled, but the name
on the marking changed during the late nineteenth
century to refer to the section of a train's route, or
run, served by a single mail car.

Up until about the 1870s, all mail handled by clerks
was date-stamped, but after this time only registered mail and letters collected from station
mailboxes were stamped on board.

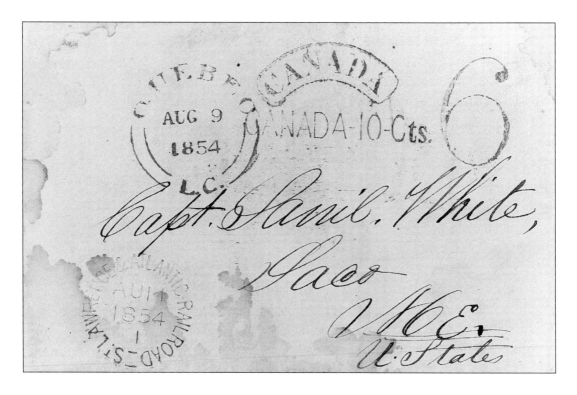

St. Lawrence and Atlantic Railroad; August 11, 1854; conductor 1; "double split ring" type. *This postmark is historically significant because it represents the first railway in Canada that date-stamped mail. The practice was introduced in 1853 for mail carried on board. The amount of postage owing on this letter has been marked with numerical handstamps. The letter was folded back on itself to form a cover and was sealed with red wax before being posted at Québec.*

Courtesy of William Robinson, Vancouver, British Columbia

NOTE: The quality of the reproduction of these markings varies, depending on how clearly the original marking was made.

Envelopes bearing the markings of the date stamp and other instruments are avidly sought by collectors today. Many philatelists specialize in collecting and studying the wide range of date-stamp styles. One of the most prolific collectors, Lewis M. Ludlow, has organized these marks into thirty-five types and has subdivided each type into additional categories.[71] Ludlow has documented approximately 200 variations in date-stamp appearance from 1853 to 1971. This number does not include "Registered" date stamps or those bearing the name of a mail clerk and does not, of course, take into consideration all the different names of railway post offices which would have shared a common design style.

This chapter reproduces some examples of railway post office date stamps on envelopes, organized according to chronology. This survey is intended as a brief introduction to the postmarks applied by railway mail clerks. While several markings may appear on an envelope, only those relating to the railway mail service have been transcribed.

Readers interested in more detailed philatelic information should refer to the bibliography for a list of some specialized literature. The library of the Canadian Postal Archives, in Ottawa, houses a wealth of information on this subject. An important resource is the Canadian Railway Post Office Study Group of the British North America Philatelic Society. Devoted members of this group are largely responsible for the accomplishments to date in the documentation of railway postmarks.

Ontario, Simcoe and Huron Railroad; April 18, 1855; "split ring" type. *In 1854, this railroad was one of the first in Canada to outfit a train with a post office so that postal workers could sort mail on board. The black border and wax seal indicate that the letter inside announces someone's death. The envelope travelled by packet boat to England.*

Courtesy of William Robinson, Vancouver, British Columbia

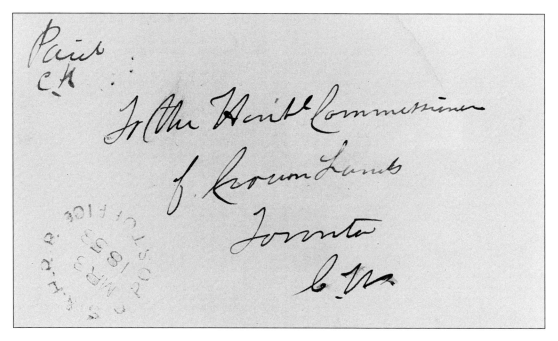

Ontario, Simcoe and Huron Union Railroad post office; March 3, 1858; "split ring" type. *Prepayment of postage has been indicated by pen. The letter is addressed to Toronto in Canada West. Prior to the common use of postage stamps, the postmaster wrote "Paid" in the corner to indicate prepayment of postage.*

Courtesy of William Robinson, Vancouver, British Columbia

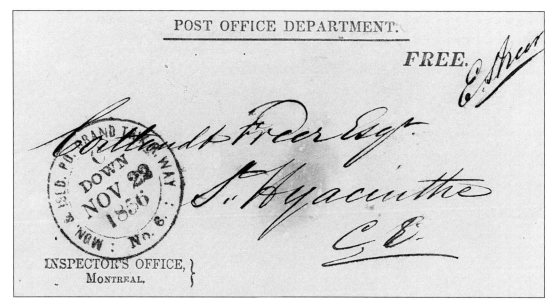

Montréal and Island Pond, Grand Trunk Railway; mail clerk 6; November 22, 1856; train "C"; direction "down"; large "double circle" type. *The envelope contained post office correspondence and therefore travelled postage-free to Saint-Hyacinthe in Canada East.*

Courtesy of William Robinson, Vancouver, British Columbia

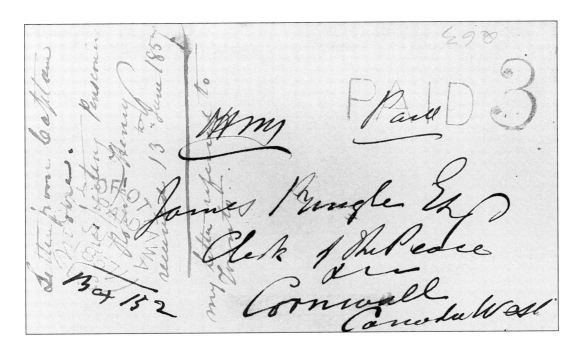

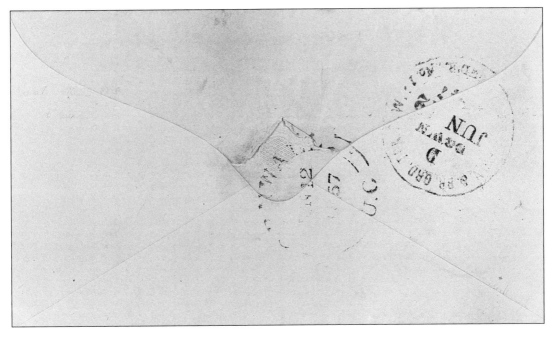

Montréal and Brockville, Grand Trunk Railway; mail conductor No. 1; train "D"; direction "down"; June 12, 1857; large "double circle" type. *Prepayment of postage has been marked in red with a numerical handstamp, along with the City of Ottawa, Upper Canada, postmark. Both sides of the envelope are shown.*

Courtesy of William Robinson, Vancouver, British Columbia

Montréal and Island Pond, Grand Trunk Railway; mail clerk 5; May 10, 1858; train "A"; direction "up"; large "double circle" type. *The imperforate, three-pence "beaver" postage stamp has been cancelled with a pen mark and "Paid" has been written in red in the other corner, for additional emphasis.*

Courtesy of William Robinson, Vancouver, British Columbia

Montréal and Island Pond, Grand Trunk Railway; mail clerk 5; February 11, 1860; train "B"; direction "down"; large "double circle" type. *The perforated, five-cent "beaver" postage stamp has been cancelled with a seven-ring obliterator.*

Courtesy of William Robinson, Vancouver, British Columbia

Quebec and Richmond Section, Grand Trunk Railway; mail clerk 1; night, April 14, 1870; "double outer circle, single inner circle" type. *The date stamp has been used to cancel the two three-cent "small Queen Victoria" postage stamps.*

Courtesy of William Robinson, Vancouver, British Columbia

On this "End of Track" envelope, the origin of posting is identified only by the return address stamped onto the envelope: Care of C. P. Mail Company, End of Track, Canadian Pacific Railway, via Calgary, Canada. The date is known by the postmark on the back side, August 31, 1884, applied when the letter arrived at the Saint John, New Brunswick, post office. The three-cent stamp has been cancelled using a cork obliterator.

Courtesy of William Robinson, Vancouver, British Columbia

End of Track, British Columbia, Canadian Pacific Railway; June 25, 1885. *This very rare postmark was applied when the letter was sent from the office of James Ross, Manager of Construction of the Canadian Pacific Railway, Mountain Division. Very few envelopes marked with this date stamp have survived over the years.*

Courtesy of William Robinson, Vancouver, British Columbia

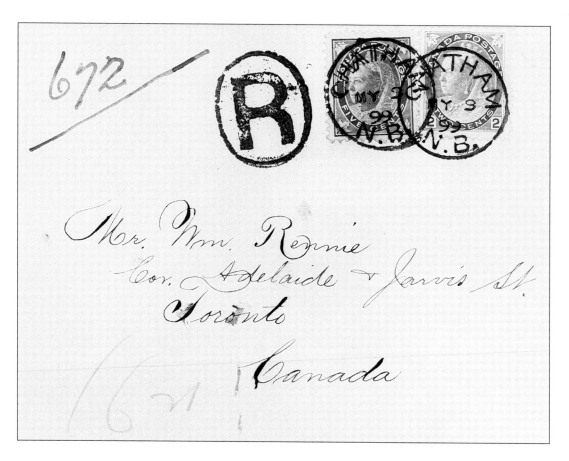

This letter was sent by registered mail from Chatham, New Brunswick, in 1899. By this time, railway mail clerks were only date-stamping registered mail and letters collected en route.

Moncton and Campbellton postal car; north; May 9, 1899. *The marking ties the flap to the back of the envelope, as was the custom with registered mail. Both sides of the envelope are shown.*

Courtesy of Ron Kitchen, Ottawa, Ontario

Grand Trunk Railway, Winnipeg and Rivers R.P.O.; mail clerk 1; train 2; March 29, 1915. *This postcard was mailed at the train station or directly onto the mail car.*

Courtesy of Ron Kitchen, Ottawa, Ontario

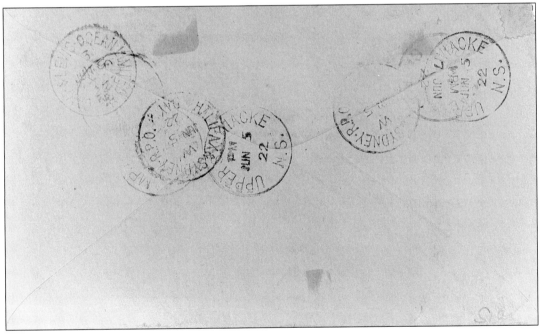

Halifax and Sydney R.P.O.; day; west; June 5, 1922. Campbellton and Lévis Ocean Limited; train 3; June 6, 1922. *This letter was sent by registered mail from Upper Stewiacke Pool, Nova Scotia. The postage stamps have been cancelled by an eight-bar obliterator. Both sides of the envelope are shown.*

Courtesy of Ron Kitchen, Ottawa, Ontario

St. John's and Port aux Basques R.P.O, Newfoundland; train Express 1; June 19, 1933. *This was posted at the train station or directly onto the mail car.*

Courtesy of Ron Kitchen, Ottawa, Ontario

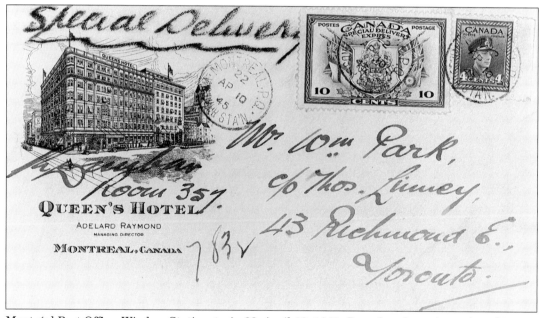

Montréal Post Office, Windsor Station; train 22; April 10, 1945. *Posted at the train station, this special-delivery letter could have been sent by a railway mail clerk staying at the Queen's Hotel, where out-of-town clerks sometimes stayed.*

Courtesy of Ron Kitchen, Ottawa, Ontario

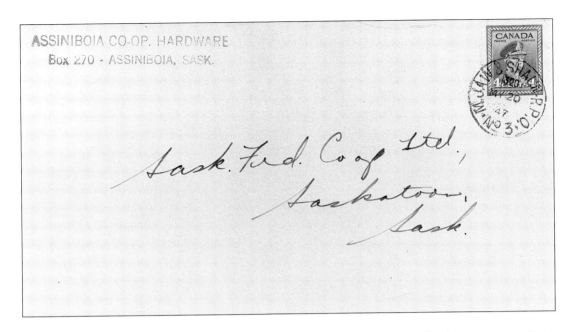

Moose Jaw and Shaunavon R.P.O.; mail clerk 3; train 320; May 20, 1947. *This letter was posted at the train station or directly onto the mail car.*

Courtesy of Ron Kitchen, Ottawa, Ontario

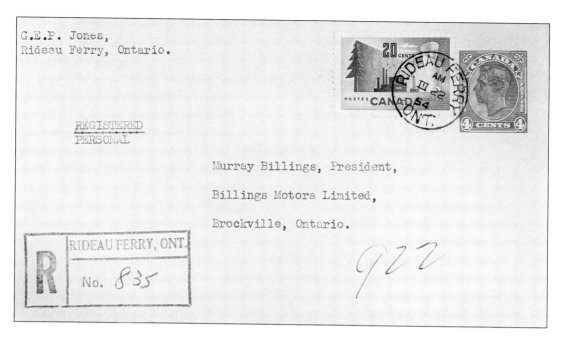

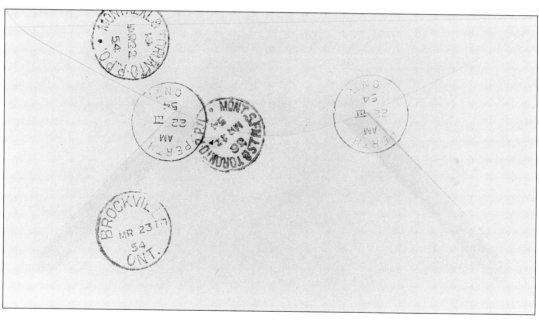

Montréal and Toronto R.P.O.; train 19; March 22, 1954. *This was sent by registered mail from Rideau Ferry, Ontario. Both sides of the envelope are shown.*
Courtesy of Ron Kitchen, Ottawa, Ontario

Toronto, Stratford and London R.P.O.; train 20; October 4, 1964. *The first run of this train is acknowledged on the envelope.*

Courtesy of William Robinson, Vancouver, British Columbia

The last run of the Montréal and Toronto R.P.O. on April 24, 1971, is commemorated on this souvenir envelope. Railway mail clerk Michael Millar added his own handstamp to the cluster of postmarks around the border, which document earlier R.P.O.s running out of Montréal.

Courtesy of William Robinson, Vancouver, British Columbia

This souvenir cover displays the special flag cancellation applied by the Perfect machine.

Courtesy of Edith L. Harlick, Richmond Hill, Ontario

Photograph by Steve Darby

The Royal Train

The first royal tour of Canada by a reigning monarch was a major historic—and philatelic—event. When King George VI of England and Queen Elizabeth toured Canada in 1939, they travelled by train. A railway post office accompanied the entourage, not only to process the Royal correspondence, but to transmit the press reports sent by the corps of media covering the tour.

In preparation for the enthusiastic public reception of this historic tour, the postal car was equipped with the latest modern technology, a Perfect cancelling machine, to apply the postal cancellation to the souvenir covers that had been specially produced for the event and which were welcomed on board.

The response was impressive: about 305,000 philatelic items were handled in the mail car, half of which were First Day Covers dated May 15, 1939.[72]

Autographed cover by 1939 Royal Train postmaster, G.W. Ross. Both sides of the envelope are shown.

National Postal Museum 1974.1078.5

Photographs by Steve Darby

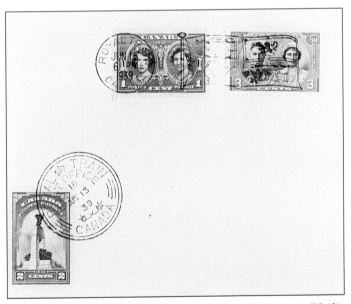

In 1951, when Queen Elizabeth II and Prince Philip conducted their first tour of Canada, the Royal Train was brought out of storage. This time, souvenir philatelic mail was refused on board. Though forbidden, many philatelic covers did manage to sneak into the mail car to receive the coveted Royal Train postmark.

National Postal Museum circular date stamp used on the 1951 Royal Train and date-type box bearing the impression of the postmark

National Postal Museum 1974.1079.7, 1974.1079.6

Photograph by Steve Darby

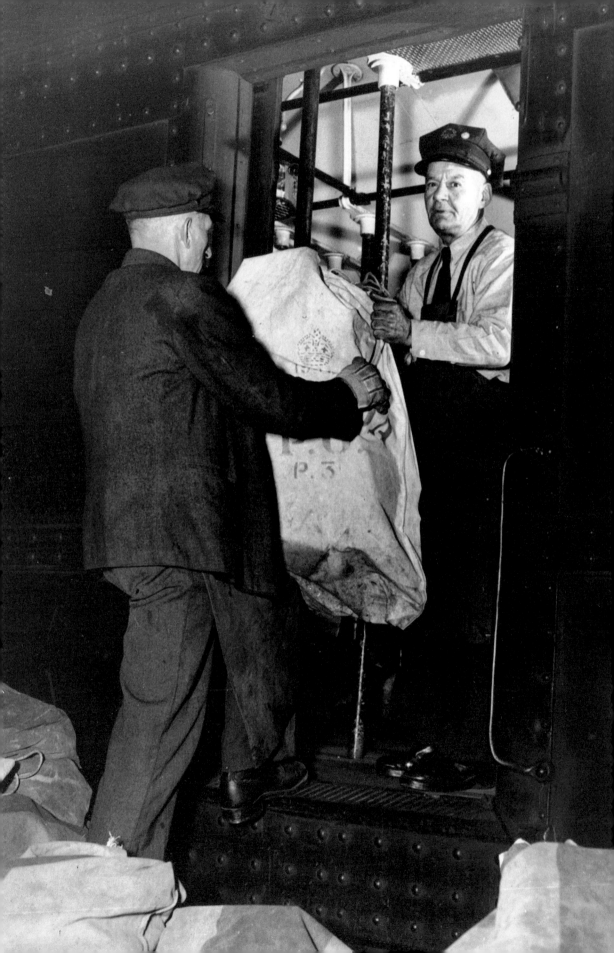

Conclusion

> To tell the story of the Canadian Postal Service is
> to tell the story of Canada itself, because from the
> days of the earliest pioneers the Post Office has
> kept pace with the development of the country.[73]

The Post Office has always recognized and taken
seriously the important supporting role it plays in
the theatre of our nation. Almost one hundred years
before the Postmaster General wrote those words in
his 1949 annual report, similar words appeared in
the first annual report produced in 1852 by the
Province of Canada:

> To follow and encourage, by the establishment of
> new Post routes and Offices, and of improved
> facilities upon the older routes, the rapid growth
> and settlement of the Province, is one of the most
> useful and pleasing functions of the Department,
> and no exertions have been spared to give energy
> and efficiency to this branch of its duties.[74]

The aim of this book has been to tell the story of the
railway mail service in order to recognize the important part it has played in long-distance communication during a significant portion of Canadian history.
The mail clerks have told their own stories in their
own words. And, because a picture is worth a thousand words, photographs of historical objects and
settings have been reproduced liberally to visualize
the sense of time and place.

This text does not represent the final word on the
story of the railway mail service in Canada. More
could have been said. Operations on board the postal
car could have been fleshed out in greater detail, the
historical summary could have contained more facts,
more could have been said about mail handling on

OPPOSITE PAGE:

*Transfer man, Jack Kempton,
takes on bags of mail in the
Ottawa district, circa 1950.*

*Courtesy of the National Archives
of Canada (PA 67178)*

Posing on board a mail car, circa 1910

Courtesy of the National Archives of Canada (PA 98506)

board coastal steamers, more anecdotes could have been related about life on board and, importantly, the place of this innovative form of postal handling and delivery could have been analysed in greater depth within the context of Canadian history. However, in the interest of producing for the first time a social history of the Canadian railway mail service and of appealing to a general readership, this presentation has emphasized description over analysis and has not sought to be exhaustive.

If, at times, the lens through which the railway mail service has been viewed seems rose-tinted, yielding a nostalgic and romanticized image, this is because of the highly subjective nature of oral testimony. The recollections of former railway mail clerks are bound to be biased in favour of fond memories and glorification, as is normal with anyone invited to reminisce about days gone by. The strength of oral history is that it can speak with a human voice where official documents are silent, and can provide a counterpoint to "official" history by revealing the unofficial context in which the documents were created.

Many readers probably remember something of the railway mail service era. Maybe you watched the mail train pull into the station in your hometown. Maybe a relative who worked in the post office or on board trains during the days of the railway mail service spoke of it. Maybe you recall receiving letters date-stamped with a railway post-office mark. Whatever the source of information, the picture you had of the railway mail service was probably sketchy. It is hoped that this book has provided the colour with which to transform that sketch into a vibrant and animated picture.

Appendix

ORAL SOURCES

Former railway mail clerks who were interviewed on audiotape, including the years they worked as mail clerks, their place of residence, and the date they were interviewed. They are listed by province, from east to west, in the order in which they were interviewed.

Edwin Cranford	(1945-1968)	Harbour Grace	Newfoundland	7/03/87
Edgar Skanes	(1946-1968)	St. John's	Newfoundland	8/03/87
Guy Rousnefell	(1913-1946)	Halifax	Nova Scotia	4/03/87
Frank C. Peebles	(1945-1971)	Halifax	Nova Scotia	4/03/87
Clarence J. Tobin	(1944-1967)	Halifax	Nova Scotia	5/03/87
William D. Earle	(1954-1971)	Halifax	Nova Scotia	5/03/87
Leo P. Gormley	(1948-1968)	Saint John	New Brunswick	2/03/87
J. Stanley Smith	(1947-1969)	Saint John	New Brunswick	2/03/87
William F. Cody	(1947-1971)	Saint John	New Brunswick	2/03/87
J. Donald McDermott	(1945-1969)	Saint John	New Brunswick	3/03/87
Jean-Marc Taillon	(1948-1961)	Québec	Quebec	9/02/87
Roger Picard	(1948-1952)	Sainte-Foy	Quebec	9/02/87
Louis-Phillipe Renaud	(1937-1970)	Charlesbourg	Quebec	10/02/87
Louis-Phillipe Pressé	(1947-1971)	Québec	Quebec	11-12/02/87
Joseph E.A. Morin	(1946-1970)	Sainte-Foy	Quebec	12/02/87
Wilbrod Ross	(1946-1971)	Sillery	Quebec	13/02/87
Edmond-Louis Maltais	(1938-1961)	Beauport	Quebec	13/02/87
Paul Sarault	(1952-1958)	Hull	Quebec	26/02/87
Albert Duchesneau	(1928-1958)	Québec	Quebec	28/03/87
Lionel Bouthillier	(1936-1969)	Montréal	Quebec	28/03/87
Irénée Gagnon	(1937-1964)	Montréal	Quebec	28/03/87
Harry Crouch	(1921-1957)	Ottawa	Ontario	27/02/87
Albert Ryan	(1941-1950)	Nepean	Ontario	27/02/87
Milton Wilkins	(Postmaster, Royal Tour, 1951)	Ottawa	Ontario	27/02/87
Gordon R. Storey	(1944-1969)	London	Ontario	5/03/87
Ronald G. Dickie	(1943-1968)	London	Ontario	5/03/92
Bruce F. Greenway	(1949-1965)	London	Ontario	5/03/87
Harold Victor Holland	(1946-1949)	London	Ontario	6/03/87
Harold T. Elgie	(1942-1964)	London	Ontario	6/03/87
W.M. Abdallah	(1949-1951)	Komoka	Ontario	6/03/87
Norman W. Verner	(1918-1965)	Hamilton	Ontario	7/03/87
Michael Millar	(1965-1971)	Barrie	Ontario	8/03/87
Paul-Emile Bourassa	(1946-1971)	Scarborough	Ontario	9/03/87
W.T. Cooper	(1952-1970)	Toronto	Ontario	9/03/87
David C. Blackhall	(1950-1970)	Toronto	Ontario	9/03/87
Robert Strachan	(1946-1966)	Winnipeg	Manitoba	19/03/87
Stanley A. Martin	(1947-1966)	Winnipeg	Manitoba	19/03/87
Peter N. Shea	(1944-1967)	Winnipeg	Manitoba	19/03/87
W.G. Wolfson	(1947-1965)	Winnipeg	Manitoba	20/03/87
Orval Gittins	(1949-1965)	Burnaby	B.C.	16/03/87
Norman Johnston	(1948-1965)	Vancouver	B.C.	16/03/87
Reginald Wilfrid Wakelin	(1940-1965)	Vancouver	B.C.	16/03/87
R.J. Keron	(1917-1945)	Vancouver	B.C.	17/03/87
William James Manning	(1948-1965)	North Van.	B.C.	17/03/87

Former railway mail clerks who were interviewed on videotape during March, 1987, including the years they worked as mail clerks and their place of residence. They are listed in alphabetical order, by province, from east to west.

Paul Emile Jobin	(1954-1963)	Québec, Quebec
Robert Shannon	(1943-1971)	Saint-Romuald, Quebec
Edward A. Cybulski	(1942-1971)	Ottawa, Ontario
A.L. Humphries	(1949-1970)	Dundas, Ontario
Ken Ivison	(1932-1971)	Lynden, Ontario
Donald McCarthy	(1958-1971)	Ottawa, Ontario
John J. Miller	(1944-1971)	Hamilton, Ontario
G.W. Harvey	(1937-1957)	Winnipeg, Manitoba
Alex Koster	(1947-1965)	Winnipeg, Manitoba
Eugene LaRivière	(1945-1971)	Winnipeg, Manitoba
J.H. Longstaffe	(1944-1971)	Winnipeg, Manitoba
Les Palmer		Winnipeg, Manitoba
Les Williams		Winnipeg Manitoba

Former railway mail clerks who provided consultations and written testimonies, 1987-1990

Ken Buffett	(1958-1970)	North Bay, Ontario
David Calderwood	(1946-1956)	Ottawa, Ontario
Bernard Desparois	(1945-1966)	Hull, Quebec
A.J. Janssens	(1943-1971)	Winnipeg, Manitoba
J.B. Mooney	(1930-1965)	Québec, Quebec
Karl Remus	(1946-1949)	Ottawa, Ontario
Donald Rutherford	(1948-1954)	Ottawa, Ontario

Notes

1. In 1967, the name of the report was changed to the *Annual Report of Canada Post Office* and in 1981 it was changed to the *Canada Post Corporation Annual Report*.

2. L.F. Gillam in his books *A History of Canadian R.P.O.s* (1967) and *Canadian Mail by Rail 1836-1867* (1985) provides a detailed description of the building of this historic first railway.

3. National Archives of Canada (hereafter NAC), Records of the Canadian National Railways, RG 30, Series I.B.1, Company of proprietors of the Champlain and St. Lawrence Railroad, Vol. 133, 290.

4. This information is from an article "The Post Office and the Railroad," *British American Magazine*, 1863, National Library of Canada, microfiche F CC-4, no. 23105.

5. Reported in Lewis M. Ludlow, *Catalogue of Canadian Railway Cancellations*, 1982. An earlier postal cover may yet be discovered.

6. *Annual Report of the Postmaster General for the Year Ending 31st March, 1853*, (Québec: Lovell and Lamoureux, 1854), Appendix F.

7. Postal inspector E.S. Freer reports to James Morris, Postmaster General of Canada East, in a letter dated August 20, 1853, that this is the case along the Montréal-Island Pond line. NAC, Records of the Post Office Department, RG 3, vol. 1008, file 1853.

8. *Annual Report of the Postmaster General for the Year Ended 31st March, 1854.* (Québec: Lovell and Lamoureux, 1855), 89.

9. In a letter dated May 20, 1856, addressed to the Postmaster General (Robert Spence), the Managing Director of the Great Western Railway (C.J. Brydges) documents that his railway began carrying mails on April 1, 1854, in "distributing cars" manned by a total of six post office clerks daily. NAC, Records of the Post Office Department, RG 3, vol. 1008, file 1856.

10. Letter sent to E.S. Freer, Post Office Inspector, January 26, 1855, NAC, Records of the Post Office Department, RG 3, vol. 1008, file 1855.

11. NAC Records of the Post Office Department, RG 3, vol. 1008, file 1854, (C 137216).

12. *Annual Report of the Postmaster General for the Year Ended 31st March, 1856.* (Toronto: John Lovell, 1857), 9-10.

13. NAC, Records of the Post Office Department, RG 3, vol. 1008, file 1857.

14. *Report of the Postmaster General for the Half Year Ended 30th September, 1856, and for the Year Ended 30th September, 1857*. (Toronto: John Lovell, 1858), 11-12.

15. *Report of the Postmaster General for the Year Ending 30th September, 1859*. (Quebec: Thompson and Company, 1860), 5.

16. Statistics contained in a letter from C.J. Brydges, Managing Director of the Grand Trunk Railway to M.H. Foley, Postmaster General, November 26, 1862. National Library of Canada, microfiche F CC-4, no. 48330.

17. NAC, Records of the Post Office Department, RG 3, vol. 1008, file 1861, letter from Robert Sinclair to W.H. Griffin, Deputy Postmaster General, March 22, 1861.

18. NAC, Records of the Post Office Department, RG 3, vol. 1008, file 1863, "An Act Respecting

Railway Postal Service", Bill No. 196, 2nd Session, 7th Parliament, 26 Victoria *(sic)*, 1863.

19. Documented in a letter from W.H. Griffin, Deputy Postmaster General, to Robert Spence, Postmaster General, July 7, 1857. NAC, Records of the Post Office Department, RG 3, vol. 1008, file 1857.

20. Letters documenting this dispute can be found at the NAC, Records of the Post Office Department, RG 3, vol. 1008 and 1009.

21. *Report of the Postmaster General for the Year Ending 30th June, 1868.* (Ottawa: Hunter, Rose and Co., 1869), 2.

22. *Report of the Postmaster General for the Year Ending June 30th, 1875.* (Ottawa: MacLean, Roger and Co., 1876), 11.

23. *Report of the Postmaster General for the Year Ending 30th June, 1876.* (Ottawa: MacLean, Roger and Co., 1877) xii.

24. Information from a Post Office Department memo written by Arthur Webster, Secretary, in 1925. National Postal Museum research files.

25. *Ibid.*

26. *Report of the Postmaster General for the Year Ending June 30th, 1886.* (Ottawa: MacLean, Roger and Co., 1887), vi.

27. *Report of the Postmaster General for the Year Ended 30th June, 1889.* (Ottawa: Brown Chamberlin, 1890), xiii-xv.

28. *Report of the Postmaster General for the Year Ended June 30th, 1897.* (Ottawa: S.E. Dawson, 1898), Appendix J.

29. Post Office memo written by Arthur Webster, 1925. National Postal Museum research files.

30. *Report of the Postmaster General for the Year Ended March 31, 1913.* (Ottawa: C.H. Parmelee, 1913), Appendix L.

31. Order-in-Council No. 211, January 27, 1914.

32. Described in an article by H.A. Clarke, National Secretary of the Dominion Railway Mail Clerks' Federation, in the magazine, *The Railway Mail Clerk*, Volume 37, September, 1958.

33. Post Office memo written by Arthur Webster, 1925. National Postal Museum research files.

34. From H.A. Clarke's article in *The Railway Mail Clerk*, Volume 37, September, 1958.

35. *Report of the Postmaster General for the Year Ended 31st March, 1951.* (Ottawa: Post Office Department), 21.

36. *Report of the Postmaster General for the Year Ended March 31, 1951.* (Ottawa: Post Office Department), 20.

37. *Report of the Postmaster General, Part 1, for the Fiscal Year Ended March 31, 1952.* (Ottawa: Post Office Department), 7.

38. *Report of the Postmaster General for the Year Ending March 31, 1961.* (Ottawa: Post Office Department), 52.

39. *Annual Report of the Canada Post Office for the Year Ended March 31, 1965.* (Ottawa: Post Office Department), 36.

40. *Annual Report of the Canada Post Office for the Year Ended March 31st, 1967.* (Ottawa: Post Office Department), 9.

41. *Annual Report of the Canada Post Office for the Year Ended March 31st, 1967.* (Ottawa: Post Office Department), 25.

42. Information recorded during an oral history interview with Wilbrod Ross, Sillery, Quebec, February 13, 1987.

43. Information received during a series of oral history interviews conducted by the National Postal Museum with former Canada Post postmasters during 1990.

44. NAC, Records of the Post Office Department, RG 3, vol. 1152, p. 21, (C 137218).

45. NAC, Records of the Post Office Department, RG 3, vol. 1152, p. 97, (C 137224).

46. *Report of the Postmaster General for the Year Ended 30th June, 1890.* (Ottawa: Brown Chamberlin, 1891), ix.

47. The project was undertaken by Stadaconé Inc., Sainte-Foy, Quebec, under contract to the National Postal Museum. The interviews, recorded on either audio- or videotape, along with a written inventory of their contents, are housed at the National Postal Museum. The names of the railway mail clerks and the dates of their interviews are listed in the Appendix.

48. NAC, Records of the Department of Transport, RG 12, Series A.1, Central Registry Files, vol. 2022, file 3910-5, pt. 1.

49. Described in a letter to the National Postal Museum dated January 30, 1987. Mr. Janssens was a mail clerk on branch lines in the Winnipeg District from 1943 to 1971.

50. NAC, Records of the Post Office Department, RG 3, vol. 1008, file 1857.

51. NAC, Records of the Post Office Department, RG 3, vol. 1152, p. 130, (C 137225).

52. NAC, Records of the Post Office Department, RG 3, vol. 1152, p. 76, (C 137222).

53. Correspondence dating from 1967, NAC, Records of the Post Office Department, RG 3, Accession 90-91/005, Box 240, file 93-2-23, "Catch bags, 1937-1967." Additional correspondence in file 108-2-1, Canada Post Corporation dormant records, documents the manufacture of catchpost bags by inmates at the Kingston Penitentiary in 1959 (copies in the National Postal Museum research files).

54. Letter from P.G. Bucke, Post Office Inspector, to Alexander Campbell, Postmaster General, October 6, 1870. NAC, Records of the Post Office Department, RG 3, vol. 1009.

55. NAC, Records of the Post Office Department, RG 3, vol. 1152, p. 48, (C 137221).

56. Controller, Railway Mail Service, *Instructions to Railway Mail Clerks*. (Ottawa: 1910), 31.

57. Post Office Department, *You and Your Post Office*. (Ottawa: Edmond Cloutier, 1952), 26.

58. Hiring requirements and other information related to employment in the railway mail service are contained in the *Instructions to Railway Mail Clerks* handbook that was written in 1857 and updated in 1906, 1910, 1920 and 1955. (No updates have been found for the years between 1857 and 1906.)

59. Hiring qualifications laid out in *You and Your Post Office* (Canada Post Office, 1952) stipulate that the post of railway mail clerk is "open to male postal employees..."

60. Extract from a letter to the National Postal Museum dated January 30, 1987. Mr. Janssens was a mail clerk on branch lines in the Winnipeg district from 1943 to 1971.

61. NAC, Records of the Post Office Department, RG 3, vol. 2747, file 115.

62. *Postmaster General Report for the Year Ended 30th June, 1898.* (Ottawa: S.E. Dawson, 1899), Appendix J, 5.

63. NAC, Records of the Department of Transport, RG 12, Series A.1, Central Registry Files, vol. 2022, file 3910-5, pt. 1.

64. Controller, Railway Mail Service, *Instructions to Railway Mail Clerks*. (Ottawa, 1906) 13.

65. NAC, Records of the Post Office Department, RG 3, vol. 1152, p. 79, (C 137223).

66. Information contained in a letter written by Paul Bégin on behalf of J.B. Mooney, dated February 14, 1987, addressed to the National Postal Museum.

67. NAC, Records of the Post Office Department, RG 3, vol. 2747, file 115, (C 137217).

68. *Manual of Instructions for Railway Mail Clerks.* (Ottawa: Post Office Department, 1955), 2.

69. Reported in Dave Brown's column "Below the Hill," *The Ottawa Journal*, Tuesday, March 5, 1974.

70. Extract from the manuscript, "General Instructions for Railway Mail Clerks", NAC, Records of the Post Office Department, RG 3, vol. 1008, file Railway Mail 1857.

71. Lewis M. Ludlow, *Catalogue of Canadian Railway Cancellations*, 1982. For full bibliographic information and for the names of other catalogues, please refer to the Bibliography.

72. Recorded in Lewis M. Ludlow, *Catalogue of Canadian Railway Cancellations*, (Tokyo: 1982), 199.

73. *Report of the Postmaster General for the Year Ended March 31, 1949.* (Ottawa: Post Office Department), 13.

74. *Annual Report of the Postmaster General, for the Year Ending 5th April, 1852.* (Québec: John Lovell, 1852), Appendix V.

Select Bibliography

PRIMARY SOURCES

Most of the archival information for this book was drawn from the Post Office Department records, which are housed in Record Group 3 at the National Archives of Canada. In this record group, volumes numbered 1008, 1009, 2240, 2246, 3290, 3291 contained particularly useful information on the railway mail service.

In addition to the Archives, works published by Canada Post Office over the last 140 years provided a rich source of information, particularly these:

POST OFFICE DEPARTMENT. *Annual Report of the Postmaster General* for the years 1851 to 1971. (See endnote 1.)

POST OFFICE DEPARTMENT. *Instructions to Railway Mail Clerks, 1857, 1906, 1910, 1920, 1955.*

POST OFFICE DEPARTMENT. *You and Your Post Office.* Ottawa: Edmond Cloutier, 1952.

POST OFFICE DEPARTMENT. *Specifications for Mail Cars.* 1919, 1936.

SECONDARY SOURCES

CLARKE, H. A. "The Railway Mail Service of Canada, the Railway Mail Clerks' Federation." *The Civil Service Review* (December 1946).

CLARKE, H. A. "The Railway Mail Service of Canada, the Canadian Railway Mail Clerks' Federation, the Past, the Present, the Future." *The Railway Mail Clerk* 37 (September 1958).

GILLAM, L. F. *A History of Canadian R.P.O.s.* Osset, England: S. Cockburn and Son Ltd., 1967.

GILLAM, L. F. *Canadian Mail by Rail 1836-1867.* Rotherham, England: Richard Printing Co., 1985.

LEGGETT, ROBERT. *Railways of Canada*. Newton Abbot: David and Charles, 1973.

LUDLOW, LEWIS M. *Catalogue of Canadian Railway Cancellations*. Tokyo: Lewis M. Ludlow, 1982.

MCLEOD O'REILLY, SUSAN. "Remembering the Railway Post Office." Unpublished research document, National Postal Museum, 1987.

POST OFFICE DEPARTMENT. "A Tribute to the Railway Mail Service." *Communications '71*, no. 9, 1971.

SHAW, T.P.G. *The Handbook and Catalogue of Canadian Transportation Postmarks*. Royal Philatelic Society of Canada: 1963.

STADACONÉ INC. *Inventaire de la collection d'enquêtes orales auprès des commis-ambulants*. (Inventory of the collection of oral interviews with railway mail clerks.) Sainte-Foy: 1987.

STADACONÉ INC. *Rapport-synthèse du projet d'enquêtes orales auprès des commis-ambulants*. (Summary report of oral interviews with railway mail clerks.) Sainte-Foy: 1987.

WEBSTER, Arthur. "Mail Service by Railway." Ottawa: Post Office Department, circa 1925. (A copy of the manuscript is in the National Postal Museum research files.)

Susan McLeod O'Reilly

is curator at the National Postal Museum. She curated **On Track: The Railway Mail Service in Canada**, as well as smaller exhibitions for the Museum, and for Parks Canada and the National Capital Commission. She has worked as an interpretive planner at the Royal Ontario Museum, and as an archaeologist. She has an undergraduate degree in archaeology/anthropolgy from Trent University and a Master's degree in museum studies from the University of Toronto.